JourneyThrough®

Matthew

62 Biblical Insights by **Mike Raiter**

Foreword

The gospel of Matthew is a book about Jesus, whose name means Saviour. Matthew tells us that this Jesus is Immanuel, God with us. He is the Son of God and Son of David, the long-awaited Messiah and King of the Jews, who fulfils all of God's promises to Israel. He is Rabbi, the world's greatest teacher, and He is Lord, the One who calls everyone, everywhere to follow Him. Above all, Matthew shows us the King who dies and rises again so we can be His people.

The Lord Jesus we meet in these pages is a Master who is gentle and compassionate, but also uncompromising in His demand for obedience to the will of God. He expects nothing less than a "greater righteousness", which is obeying the Lord with both the desires of the heart and the deeds of the life. At the same time, Jesus provides us with all the resources we need to live a life that honours and glorifies God.

While the primary focus of Jesus' ministry according to Matthew is first-century Israel, his gospel is full of wonderful and challenging lessons about what it means for us to live as disciples of Jesus Christ today. There are teachings on family relationships, church life, money, dealing with conflict, and so much more.

Journey with Matthew and meet King Jesus, who rules with all authority.

To God be the glory,
Mike Raiter

We're glad you've decided to join us on a journey into a deeper relationship with Jesus Christ!

For over 50 years, we have been known for our daily Bible reading notes, *Our Daily Bread*. Many readers enjoy the pithy, inspiring, and relevant articles that point them to God and the wisdom and promises of His unchanging Word.

Building on the foundation of *Our Daily Bread*, we have developed the *Journey Through* series to help believers spend time with God in His Word, book by book. We trust this daily meditation on God's Word will draw you into a closer relationship with Him through our Lord and Saviour, Jesus Christ.

How to use this resource

READ: This book is designed to be read alongside God's Word as you journey with Him. It offers explanatory notes to help you understand the Scriptures in fresh ways.

REFLECT: The questions are designed to help you respond to God and His Word, letting Him change you from the inside out.

RECORD: The space provided allows you to keep a diary of your journey as you record your thoughts and jot down your responses.

An Overview

One day, while he was sitting in his tax collection booth, Matthew heard Jesus call, "Follow me". From then on, the reformed sinner became one of the Twelve. We have in his gospel an eyewitness account of the ministry of Jesus. The Gospels are not biographies in the modern sense of the word. They are "preached histories"—selective records of the life and work of Jesus, designed to both elicit and strengthen faith in Jesus.

Being Jewish, Matthew repeatedly emphasises how Jesus fulfilled all that was predicted of the coming Messiah. Jesus' ministry is explicitly to "the lost sheep of the house of Israel", but there are numerous indications that the day of the Gentiles is about to dawn. Jesus preaches the gospel of the kingdom of heaven, and calls people to be His disciples and live under His rule. He calls for a life of radical righteousness marked by justice, mercy, and faithfulness, while at the same time assuring His followers that His yoke is easy and His burden is light. Despite the persistent opposition of the Jewish leaders, and according to the will of God, Jesus goes to Jerusalem, where He is hailed as the Messiah, rejected, crucified, and then raised from the dead, that He might bring salvation to all who trust and obey Him.

The Structure of Matthew

1:1–4:11	Evidence for Jesus of Nazareth as the Messiah and King
4:12–7:29	The declaration of the King's standards
8:1–11:1	The authentication of the King's authority
11:2–13:53	Opposition and rejection of the King's authority
13:54–19:2	The response of the King
19:3–26:1	The formal presentation of the King to the nation and the ensuing rejection
26:2–28:20	The crucifixion and resurrection of the King

Key Verse

Simon Peter answered, "You are the Messiah, the Son of the living God."
—Matthew 16:16

Day 1

Read Matthew 1:1–17

The opening line of a book is very important, but you would not call the opening line of Matthew's gospel an attention grabber: "This is the genealogy of Jesus the Messiah the son of David, the son of Abraham . . ." (v. 1).

Historically, genealogies have revealed something of the values of a culture, and this is true of the genealogies of Israel as recorded in the Bible (e.g., 1 Chronicles 1–9). Ancient genealogies were selective, and Matthew has selected just 42 of Jesus' ancestors. He has arranged them in three groups of 14 which cover the three great epochs of Jewish history: from Abraham the patriarch to King David (vv. 1–6); from David to the exile in Babylon (vv. 7–11); and then from the exile to the coming of the true son of David, Jesus (vv. 12–16).

Do you see Matthew's main point? It is simply that Jesus is the climax of Israel's history. God is the author of history, and He will bring it to its ordained end. Jesus is the ultimate goal of history.

However, this genealogy does not just tell us who Jesus is, but why He came. In Matthew's long list of names we find the presence of four unusual women. Matthew does not record the traditional matriarchs of Israel: Sarah,

Rebekah, Rachel, and Leah. Instead, he mentions four women with Gentile backgrounds: Rahab, a Canaanite; Tamar, likely another Canaanite; then a Moabitess, Ruth; and finally Bathsheba, the wife of a non-Jew, Uriah the Hittite (see 2 Samuel 11:3). Some Bible scholars believe that by marrying outside of her race, Bathsheba, although born a Jew, became a Gentile as a result.

By providing this list of names, Matthew is preaching the gospel to us. **God's salvation is for men and women. The good news is for all people, both Jew and Gentile. God's ultimate plan is to form a people for himself from all nations.** The overarching theme is clear: all of history will find its fulfilment in the eventual plan and purpose of God. Just as He brought the first stage of history to its ordained climax, so He will guide the next. Again, the climax will be the coming of Jesus!

This is very comforting. These opening words of Matthew's gospel remind us that God is sovereign. His salvation plan embraces all of mankind, regardless of race or gender, and in carrying out His plan He can use anyone He deems fit, just like these four women.

ThinkThrough

Think about these four women (Tamar, Rahab, Ruth, and Bathsheba). What does their place in Jesus' genealogy say about the way God works? How might they be preparing us for the next woman in our story: Mary, the mother of Jesus?

Sometimes we may think that the world is in chaos and wonder what the future holds. What comfort can we draw for our lives today from Matthew's brief survey of history?

Day 2

Read Matthew 1:18–25

Sadly, many in today's world take the making of promises too lightly. In reality, it is a serious thing. This account of the birth of Jesus shows God keeping a mighty promise.

We meet here the young couple, Joseph and Mary. They have recently become engaged, and in ancient Israel that was as legally binding as marriage. Therefore, on discovering Mary is pregnant (Joseph does not yet know it is by the Holy Spirit), Jewish, Greek, and Roman law all demand that he publicly divorce her. However, Joseph resolves to do it as discreetly as possible (v. 19). He wants to minimise any scandal and protect her reputation. Joseph is a righteous man, which means he understands that grace and mercy are more important than strict adherence to the law.

Then Matthew tells us who this child really is. Shortly after King Ahaz ascended the throne in 735 BC, God promised that He would protect Judah, which was being threatened by her godless neighbours, and He would give her a sign: a virgin would have a baby boy and she would call him Immanuel. This name would be a reminder that God would be with His people and save them (Isaiah 7:14).

Now we fast forward 730 years and a baby is born. But this child really was "God with us". "Immanuel" was not just a name; in this child God physically came among us.

By His Spirit, Jesus is still with us. Now, wherever we go, God will be with us. Whatever happens, God will be with us. **But Jesus will not just be with us here and now, He will also be with us on the day when we will need Him most.** This child was not just Immanuel; He was "Jesus", which means "he will save his people from their sins" (v. 21). Everyone will have to stand before God the righteous judge one day (Hebrews 9:27). We need someone who will be with us and say to our heavenly Father, "I have paid the price for their sins. I stand with them." Jesus, Immanuel, will turn to us and say, "Today you will be with me in paradise." God with us forever!

ThinkThrough

Read Matthew 28:20. Just before He left for heaven, what did Jesus tell His disciples? Are there times in your life when you have been very conscious of God being with you?

We don't learn much about Joseph in the Gospels, but verse 19 tells us he was a very godly man. What can you learn about his character from this passage? What can you learn from how he treats Mary?

Day 3

Read Matthew 2:1–12

Matthew 2 opens shortly after Jesus' birth. Although Joseph's home and business are in Nazareth, the family are currently in Bethlehem. While there, wise men, or magi, visit Him. Matthew does not tell us how many came (in some Christian traditions there were as many as 12 magi!). They come from the East, perhaps Babylon.

The "magi" are important and influential members of the royal court, experts in science, mathematics, history, and astronomy. They have seen some new appearance in the sky which, they believe, heralds an event of cosmic significance, the birth of a great king. Perhaps they knew of Numbers 24:17, reading from the Septuagint, the Greek translation of the Old Testament: "A star shall rise out of Jacob, a man shall spring out of Israel". So they have come to Jerusalem. When they arrive, they bring news that the Jews have been waiting centuries to hear: the Messiah has come.

You would have expected God's people to rejoice, but we are told that their king, Herod, "and all Jerusalem with him" (v. 3), are troubled. How stunning! Gentiles travel thousands of miles at great cost to come and worship a foreign king, yet not one Jew would walk a few miles to greet their Messiah and Saviour.

Supernaturally, the star guides the magi to Jesus, and Isaiah's prophecy delivered 700 years ago is fulfilled: "Nations will come to your light, and kings to the brightness of your dawn . . . bearing gold and incense and proclaiming the praise of the LORD" (Isaiah 60:3, 6).

Twice in the gospel of Matthew Jesus is called the King of the Jews. Here at the beginning, and then later at His death when Herod's son, Antipas, conspires with the people to kill Jesus (Luke 13:31; 23:7–13; Acts 4:27). A sign was placed over the cross: "THE KING OF THE JEWS" (Matthew 27:37). At both His birth and death, Jews were troubled while Gentiles believed: magi worshipped Christ at His birth, while a centurion confessed at His death, "Surely he was the Son of God" (Matthew 27:54).

Nothing has changed in 2,000 years. **Some reject Jesus while others—and often the ones you would least expect—rejoice, worship, and offer Him the gift of their lives, the only appropriate gift for such a universal king.**

Why do you think that the people of Jerusalem were so disturbed at the news of the birth of their King (v. 3)? Does anything in the history of Israel prepare us for this reaction?

Think about the people you live among. How do they respond to the good news of Jesus? Why do you think people today are often troubled by the gospel? What does the response of the wise men tell us about how and why some people come to Jesus?

Day 4

Read Matthew 2:13–23

Nothing takes God by surprise. That is what we mean when we say God is sovereign. Nothing in the life of Jesus took God by surprise. It was all ordained and spoken about in the Old Testament. In Jesus, God's promises find fulfilment. In Him the shadow becomes reality.

The early life of the Lord Jesus is a story of divine guidance. Through a dream God guides Joseph to marry his fiancée, who is pregnant through the Holy Spirit (Matthew 1:20). Through a star He guides Gentile magi to come and worship the King of the nations (Matthew 2:2). Through another dream He warns them not to return to Herod (v. 12). Now through two more dreams God acts to protect His Son (vv. 13, 22). An infamously cruel despot, Herod ruthlessly tries to protect his throne and orders the murder of all small boys in Bethlehem. But nothing takes God by surprise. He directs Joseph to flee to Egypt (v. 13), and then eventually to the safety of Nazareth in Galilee (vv. 22–23).

Matthew is showing us how to read the Old Testament. Jesus taught His disciples that all the Scriptures point forward to Him (Luke 24:44). Matthew gives us more examples of this. The genealogy wonderfully made the point that Israel's history, the promises to Abraham, the kingdom under David, and the tragic exile, all pointed forward to the Lord Jesus, who is the true son and heir of Abraham, the true king, and the true Israel who returns from exile (Matthew 1:1–17). Now we see how even particular events in our Lord's life, such as the escape to Egypt and the Bethlehem massacre, were spoken of by the prophets (vv. 15, 18). The only way to rightly read the Bible is through Christ-focused lenses.

The persecution of Christians has never been as widespread as today. **Modern-day Herods still seek to destroy those they see as a threat to their power. Yet God is on the throne and nothing takes Him by surprise.** He protected Jesus so that He might fulfil His divine mission, and His guidance and timely provision enable us to complete the work He has for us.

What do we mean when we say the Old Testament points forward to the Lord Jesus? How often do you think of the Lord Jesus when you read the Old Testament?

There are over 50 million refugees in the world today. How can we appreciate this contemporary crisis, considering that the Lord Jesus himself spent His early years as a political refugee?

Day 5

Read Matthew 3:1–12

t is true that God accepts us as we are, but once we have met Him, we cannot stay the way we are. God has always been in the business of change and renewal.

We now fast-forward 30 years from chapter 2. All four gospels begin their description of Jesus' ministry by introducing John the Baptist (Mark 1:1–8; Luke 3:2–17; John 1:6–8, 15–34). After 400 years of silence, God began speaking through a new prophet who, like the prophets of old, called the people to repentance and promised someone greater to come. John even looked like an Old Testament prophet (2 Kings 1:8; Zechariah 13:4).

The Jews knew that one day their king would come and deliver them, and now John announces, "He's here!" Jesus' kingdom, however, is not geographical or political. It is not only spiritual but also dynamic. This King rules in people's hearts. This King changes and renews both His people and His creation. Therefore, the Jews must prepare themselves for Him by radically reforming how they think and behave (vv. 8–10). That is repentance, and it must be genuine. Like the prophets of old, John boldly rebuked any hypocritical Jewish leaders who wanted to be a part of what God was doing, but without heartfelt confession and repentance. Just being Jewish was not enough. This King will separate the genuine from the false, the good from the bad.

John announces two things about this King. First, He is "more powerful than I" (v. 11). There was a Rabbinic saying which went, "You are to do anything your master tells you to do, except untie his sandals." Yet, says John, "this King is so great, even that task would be too exalted for me." Secondly, He will baptise with the purifying, refining Spirit (v. 11). John's baptism cleansed the outside, but Jesus' fiery baptism cleanses the heart. What John commands, Jesus accomplishes. **Jesus both wills and enables renewal. By His Spirit, Jesus burns away anger, greed, and pride, and brings to birth love, peace, and generosity.**

The message is still the same: the King has come. The one way to receive Him is confession and repentance. Then He will turn your life around, so you can be the person God wants you to be.

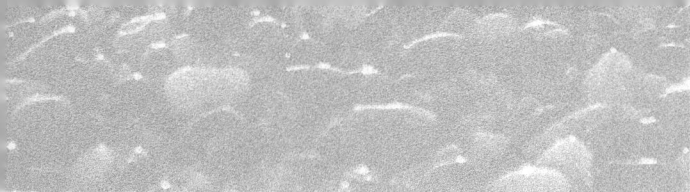

Why is John so harsh with the Jewish leaders (v. 7)? In what respects are they like the "shepherds of Israel" of the past?

Fire both purifies and consumes. How does Jesus' baptism "with the Holy Spirit and fire" express both of these features of fire? What comfort is there in these words for us? What warning can we take from them?

Day 6

Read Matthew 3:13–17

My son is a high school teacher. Recently his students told him that they like him because, "Mr. Raiter, you don't yell at us." Many teachers yell, and with some high school children, it can be hard not to yell. Nate is firm and in control, but he does not yell. The Jesus we meet in this passage will not yell at us.

John now introduces King Jesus. As His inferior, John is reluctant to baptise Jesus (vv. 13–14). However, as we have seen, Jesus is the true Israel, and must identify with His people. Unlike them, He does not come confessing His sins, but He will obediently fulfil God's role for Him (v. 15). This means He stands with them in recognising their need for salvation, and He will soon die for them to achieve it.

By His baptism Jesus' ministry is launched, and God anoints Him with the Holy Spirit. It is striking that the Spirit comes in the form of a dove (v. 16). Not in the form of an eagle or a hawk, but in the shape of a creature that is a symbol of innocence, purity, weakness, poverty, and gentleness.

What a contrast! A man of such surpassing greatness that even the greatest born of women would consider it too exalted a task to untie His shoes, and yet gentleness and humility will be the hallmarks of His ministry.

Only twice does God speak in Matthew's gospel, here and at the Transfiguration (Matthew 17:1–5), and both times He preaches the same message, "This is my Son, whom I love" (Matthew 3:17; 17:5). **God is a one-sermon preacher, with one supreme message to the world: Look, listen, and love Jesus, my Son.**

This strong but gentle King is a man we can entrust our life to. Yes, He will rebuke and admonish us, but He says, "Come to me, all you who are weary and burdened, and I will give you rest . . . for I am gentle and humble in heart" (Matthew 11:28–30). Just ask denying Peter (Matthew 26:69–75) or doubting Thomas (John 20:26–28). More than that, this is a man we *must* entrust our lives to. We are God's children, but only Jesus is the unique, eternal, beloved Son of God. Him alone we worship. Him alone we preach.

"Who is Jesus?" What are the different answers people give to this question? How can we faithfully yet sensitively speak of Christ's uniqueness in a multi-faith country?

How should the fact that the Spirit comes to Jesus in the form of a dove inform and shape our ministry to the world and to the church?

Day 7

Read Matthew 4:1–11

Sometimes, in reading Matthew's gospel, we forget that it is about Jesus. For example, when reading about Jesus' temptation in the wilderness by Satan, we often quickly move to thinking about what these verses teach us about temptation in *our* lives, and how *we* can get victory over *our* temptations. While His temptation was not unlike ours, the focus is not on us but on Jesus, and how His cosmic battle with Satan had eternal implications for the world's salvation.

The same Spirit who has just empowered Jesus for ministry now leads Him into the desert. This time of trial is part of God's necessary preparation of His Son to fulfil His ordained mission. Once again we see Jesus fulfilling Israel's history. Just as God's "son" Israel spent 40 years being tested in the wilderness (Deuteronomy 8:1–5), so too does the true Son spend 40 days being tested. However, where Israel failed and that generation perished, Jesus obeys and demonstrates that He is the true Son who can lead His people into their true rest.

Essentially, Satan tempts Jesus to use His position and power as God's Son to satisfy His own needs and desires. Jesus sees right through Satan's deceit. In the first temptation, Jesus demonstrates that He knows His hunger is meant to teach Him to rely on God's word (vv. 2–4). Israel was given bread in the desert but lacked faith (Exodus 16). Jesus renounced bread and trusted God. In the next temptation, Jesus proves that, unlike Israel, He will trust and obey God, and not put God to the test (Exodus 17:2-7). Jesus knows that demanding miraculous signs is a mark of unbelief. Finally, again unlike Israel who bowed before a golden calf, Jesus affirms He will only worship God. Jesus will one day receive all the kingdoms of the world, but it will be through his obedience to death on a cross.

It is appropriate to learn personally from Jesus' temptation. Satan's ultimate purpose in temptation is to keep us from trusting and worshipping God. Like Jesus, our greatest weapon in our battle against Satan is Scripture (vv. 4, 7, 10). Yet we should not allow our own need to distract us from grasping how much was at stake in Jesus' temptation. **If Jesus had fallen, we would still be in our sins. A failed Messiah could not be the world's Saviour. Our eternal security rested on His earthly obedience.** Praise God for His faithfulness in the face of temptation!

What was Satan's purpose in tempting Jesus?

Jesus taught us to pray, "Lead us not into temptation." What lessons can we learn about such times of trial from this passage?

Day 8

Read Matthew 4:12–25

One popular hymn is Judson Van DeVenter's "I Surrender All". DeVenter had been struggling between developing his artistic talents and becoming a full-time evangelist. Finally, he surrendered all. He said, "A new day was ushered into my life. I became an evangelist and discovered down deep in my soul a talent hitherto unknown to me." In 1896 he published his famous hymn:

All to Jesus I surrender,
Humbly at His feet I bow,
Worldly pleasures all forsaken,
Take me, Jesus, take me now.

I surrender all,
I surrender all,
All to thee, my blessed Savior,
I surrender all.

Matthew begins his account of the Lord Jesus' public ministry by telling us of His return to Galilee. He makes His home and base of operations in Capernaum (vv. 12–13). He goes there not just because it is His home territory but, more importantly, because it also fulfils the prophecy in Isaiah 9:1–2, which states that the Messiah will begin His ministry there. And since there was a large Gentile population present, another possible reason is that it demonstrates that Jesus is Saviour of all nations, not just of the Jews. Like John the Baptist,

Jesus preached the kingdom of God, but where John had promised its coming, Jesus heralds and embodies its arrival.

Matthew now describes how the first disciples "surrender all" (vv. 20, 22). This is probably not their first encounter with Jesus (cf. John 1:35–42), but now His summons turns their lives upside down, calling on them to leave their homes, work, and family. **Jesus' disciples cannot just sit and learn; they must walk and follow.** They become the master's apprentices and learn to fish for something far more valuable than food: the hearts and lives of people (v. 19).

Jesus' threefold ministry was teaching the Scriptures, publicly proclaiming the good news, and healing (v. 23; Matthew 9:35), by which He wonderfully demonstrated that God's kingdom had broken into a hurting world.

We too have sat in darkness and heard the same call: Follow me. Every true disciple of Jesus surrenders all. Some have done it literally (Matthew 19:27), while the rest have done it potentially, ready to leave everything in order to announce and build the kingdom. We too demonstrate by word and deed that the true King has come to save and to rule.

ThinkThrough

Reflect on what Jesus' command, "Follow me", means for you personally and practically.

Matthew tells us that both sets of brothers "immediately" left everything and followed Jesus (vv. 20, 22). What do you think Matthew was trying to tell us in describing the immediacy of their response? What does that mean for our own lives of discipleship?

Day 9

Read Matthew 5:1–2

My wife loves airports. It's not the flying; it's the people. She enjoys seeing an amazing cross-section of people. Yet, for all our differences, according to the Lord Jesus, there are just two kinds of people in this world: those who are poor in spirit, and those who believe they have no need to depend on God (Matthew 5:3). There are two roads in life: an easy road, and a hard road (Matthew 7:13–14). There are two gates with two destinations: the narrow gate to eternal life, and the wide gate to destruction. There are two kinds of trees that bear two kinds of fruit: good, and bad (Matthew 7:16–17). And there are two houses built on two foundations: rock, and sand (Matthew 7:24–27).

Up on the mountain, Jesus is teaching His disciples, but the crowds are listening in (vv. 1–2). In this Sermon on the Mount (chapters 5–7), we are given a sample of the teaching of Jesus.

Matthew 4:23 gives us one of his summary statements of Jesus' ministry: *Jesus went throughout Galilee, teaching in their synagogues, preaching the good news of the kingdom, and healing every disease and sickness among the people.* If we fast forward five chapters to Matthew 9:35, we find, almost word-for-word, the very same summary statement. These summaries make the point that Jesus' ministry was essentially teaching—which includes the preaching of the gospel—and healing. The five chapters between Matthew 4:23 and 9:35 are divided into two distinct halves: first a selection of Jesus' teaching (chapters 5–7), and then a selection of His miracle working (chapters 8–9).

The Sermon on the Mount is addressed primarily to disciples (vv. 1–2), to those who have believed in Him, left everything to follow Him, and become members of His kingdom of grace and power. These are His true disciples.

It is important to remember that these words are not intended to show us how we can become members of God's kingdom. **Kingdom membership is by invitation only, and the gracious King invites all to come to Him. However, kingdom membership brings responsibilities.** God has saved us so we can live lives that glorify Him—we are "the light of the world" (Matthew 5:14)—and bless others—we are "the salt of the earth" (Matthew 5:13). In short, this sermon shows us two ways to live: the way of those who have responded to God's grace, which leads to eternal life; and

the way of those who reject the Son, which leads to destruction.

ThinkThrough

Why is it important to realise that Jesus' sermon is addressed mainly to those who are already His disciples? How does this affect the way you read and understand the sermon?

Why do you think Jesus describes the life of discipleship as a "hard road", and entrance into eternal life as being through a "narrow gate"?

Day 10

Read Matthew 5:3–12

Each of the Beatitudes, or Blessings, describes both the *identity* of Jesus' true disciples and then their *destiny*.

It is surprising when Jesus announces that the most blessed, or most favoured by God, are the poor, the mourning, the meek, the hungry and thirsty, the merciful, the pure, the peacemakers, and the persecuted. These descriptions are plain statements of fact, not commands. They are all drawn from the Old Testament's descriptions of God's faithful people, who look to the only One who can help them, especially in times of crisis (see Isaiah 61).

"Blessed are the poor in spirit" (v. 3) serves as heading for all the Beatitudes. Poverty of spirit speaks of those who recognise their essential helplessness. They lack the resources needed to change their circumstances, whether material or spiritual. Such people look to the Lord, the only One who can provide all they need. **Jesus announces that the most blessed people are those who are aware of their utter dependence on God and have a single-minded devotion to Him.**

It's important to remember that the Beatitudes are all different ways of describing the disciple of Jesus; it is the same person described from different perspectives, just like how we can describe a Christian as born again, justified, a saint, and a member of the body of Christ. You can't be one and not be the others. The disciple of Christ mourns, hungers for righteousness, and is a peacemaker.

We must not forget the final beatitude: blessed are those who are persecuted because of their allegiance to Jesus (v. 10). This is just as much a feature of the true disciple as meekness and purity of heart. God's faithful people have always been the object of abuse. Don't be surprised when the world opposes you. Indeed, be surprised if it doesn't.

It is good to be reminded of our true identity. The world either ignores God's people as being of no consequence, or actively abuses and maligns them. In the end, there is only one opinion that matters: God's. And God says His children are the truly blessed ones.

True disciples of
Jesus are described
as "poor in spirit".
In what ways are you
conscious of your
spiritual poverty?

What are the
practical marks
of someone who
hungers and thirsts
for righteousness?

Day 11

Read Matthew 5:3–12

We have been shown the identity of those whom God calls "blessed". Now, in the second part of each verse, Jesus tells us *why* they are blessed. We have seen the identity of God's people, and now Jesus announces their wonderful destiny.

Just as the descriptions of the blessed refer to every true disciple, so do the promises. It is not like one of those big annual sales that offer great discounts but only on selected merchandise. No, all these wonderful promises are for every follower of Jesus.

The first and last promises are the same: "theirs is the kingdom of heaven" (vv. 3, 10). In other words, Jesus' disciples are blessed right now because they live under the loving rule and care of God. However, the other promises are all in the future tense: "they will be comforted . . . will inherit the earth . . . will be filled" (vv. 4–6).

Of course, while these promises are yet to come, in some sense we already enjoy them in part. However, we will receive them fully at the return of Jesus, when God's kingdom shall be fully established. For example, Jesus promises that we will be comforted (v. 4), but we have already received God's comfort (2 Corinthians 1:3–4). We are told that we will inherit the earth and be called God's children (vv. 5, 9), but we know that we are already God's sons and daughters, and heirs of His kingdom (Romans 8:17). Similarly, we have already received mercy (1 Peter 2:10) and fullness (Colossians 2:10).

Let me illustrate. I have four children, three of whom live overseas. Although they are far from me, I am still their father. Of course, when we are together we can talk face to face, enjoy meals together, walk together, and play together. We are already God's children, but one day, when we are in His presence, we will come into the full experience of being a child of God.

Like tasting the entrée to a great banquet, we can enjoy now a foretaste of the wonderful destiny God has planned for His children. This sermon is both a description of God's blessed people and, implicitly, an invitation to everyone to come and enter this kingdom. God can change you and give you this precious identity and glorious destiny.

Have you begun to experience these promises of God in your life today? Can you think of some specific examples?

How can these wonderful promises of our eternal destiny sustain us through difficult times?

Day 12

Read Matthew 5:13–16

Salt is the world's oldest known food additive. It plays a critical role in maintaining our health. Without enough salt in our body, muscles will not contract, blood will not circulate, food will not digest, and the heart will not beat. Salt is essential to life.

In the same way, Jesus' disciples have a vital role to play in influencing the world for God. Jesus continues to tell us, His disciples, who we are: We are the salt of the earth (v. 13). In other words, God's people are central to all that God is doing in the world. Through His disciples God wants to bless others: to bring to them the good news that their sins are forgiven; to help the poor; and to promote justice. One of our deepest human desires is to make a lasting difference in life. Here, Jesus says that His people make an impact on the widest possible scale: You are the salt of the earth.

Moreover, you are the light of the *world* (v. 14). Again we see the global dimension of this impact. Jesus goes on to stress the importance of His disciples having such an impact. Salt by its very nature is salty. A light naturally shines. If it does not, it is useless and is thrown out. Salt and light is what we are. Salt and light is what we must be.

Of course, by "salt" and "light" Jesus means our good deeds (v. 16). He will continue to teach about living righteously for the rest of the sermon. That means our lives, in conformity to God's will, are to be full of good deeds. Why? "That they may . . . glorify your Father in heaven" (v. 16). Yes, through our good deeds God desires to bless His world, but His ultimate purpose—in this and all things—is that He might receive praise and glory.

That is why we cannot be "silent witnesses". Nobody that our lives touch will ever turn and glorify the Father in heaven unless we tell them about Him. They will never appreciate that we have been merciful to them unless we testify of God's mercy to us. When we flavour and shine, and speak of the Father, however, the world will give Him honour and praise.

"You only have to believe in Jesus." Why must a Christian do good works?

Can you think of instances where the good deeds of disciples of Jesus have led to people giving glory to the Father in heaven? How should we respond to someone who may thank or compliment us for our good deeds?

Day 13

Read Matthew 5:17–48

What do we do with the commands that Moses gave to Israel? There are all kinds of instructions—about not eating certain kinds of food, keeping the Sabbath, making sacrifices, etc. How do we interpret and apply them? Do we just ignore these parts of the timeless, inspired Word of God? Didn't Jesus say here that we cannot break even the least of these commands (v. 19)?

This is another important section of the Sermon on the Mount, and Jesus' words are foundational to understanding the Christian life, particularly how we understand and apply the Old Testament.

The answer is found in verse 17: "I have not come to abolish [the law or the prophets] but to fulfil them".

Matthew's gospel repeatedly shows us how Jesus' life fulfils the Old Testament. For example, Matthew tells us that Jesus' birth in Bethlehem fulfilled Micah 5:2. The law against murder is also fulfilled in Jesus, who reveals the true meaning and intent of this law: do not nurture anger against your brother (vv. 21–26). For adultery it is: do not harbour lust (vv. 27–28); and for divorce: God meant marriage to be permanent, do not undermine it (vv. 31–32).

Jesus dealt with the remaining examples (vv. 33–48) in the same way, revealing the true and intended meaning of God's commands to Israel.

In summary, true righteousness is a righteousness of both the heart and the life, the intention and the action, a person's character and the conduct that flows from it. Or, in Paul's words, "Love is the fulfilment of the law" (Romans 13:10). Those who love from the heart perform a righteousness greater than the Pharisees (v. 20). Their hypocritical righteousness was for display; the disciple's righteousness springs from the heart.

Jesus announces that such a disciple is "perfect" (v. 48). This does not mean sinless. The word means "whole", "complete", or mature. **The "perfect" or complete Christian has a righteousness where the outward action mirrors the inward desire.**

Perhaps you find this call to inner righteousness difficult. "I really want to love this person, but I just find bitterness rising in my heart." Jesus understands this. That is why He began His sermon, "Blessed are the poor in spirit". The God who is rich in grace gives us all the resources we need to enable us to be what we are: His salt and light.

In light of what Jesus says, how should we be reading, teaching, and applying the law of Moses?

Think about Matthew 5:38–42. How would a Pharisee interpret the command, "An eye for an eye . . ."? How should a disciple of Christ react to someone who has wronged him or her? How literally should we take Jesus' commands in verses 40 to 42? Is there an underlying principle Jesus wants us to understand?

Day 14

Read Matthew 6:1–18

A few years ago, I met a teenage daughter of an acquaintance and asked how her dad was. I will never forget her reply. She simply said, "He's evil, you know." In other words, she saw the man behind the mask. Jesus saves His most vehement attacks for the hypocrites; those who appear religiously impressive but hide the reality.

Jesus has been describing the character of true righteousness (Matthew 5:1–16). It is about motive as well as action (Matthew 5:17–48). Now He describes another feature of the truly righteous life. It is "secret" or "inner" righteousness (vv. 1–18).

For the Pharisees, righteousness was all about outward appearances. The true righteousness that Jesus called for is an inner righteousness of the heart. His disciples are to be people of integrity. That is, there must be consistency between the desires of the heart, the words of the mouth, and the deeds of the life. What you observe of me and what I really am should be one and the same.

Jesus summarises this teaching in verse 1. First, the warning: "Be careful not to practise your righteousness in front of others to be seen by them". Then the consequence: "If you do, you will have no reward from your Father in heaven". The rest of the section gives three practices that all pious Jews would have observed. Jesus speaks of giving (vv. 2–4), praying (vv. 5–8), and fasting (vv. 16–18) (and we could add: running the children's programme at church, mowing the church lawn, preaching, and singing in the worship team). Do not do these things for the praise of people.

Of course, all these activities are good things to do, but the issue here is not what you do but why you do it, and for whom. In short, discipleship is a life lived before an audience of One (vv. 4, 6, 18). God sees the deed and the intention. On the day of rewarding, it will be revealed whether we lived for the praise of God or the praise of others.

These are actually liberating truths because we are freed from the burden of seeking the approval of other people. **In the end, others' estimation of us is not what really matters. All that matters is the praise of God.**

In an earlier passage, Jesus said that we should do our good deeds so people can see them and praise our Father in heaven (Matthew 5:16). Here He tells us not to perform our deeds before people. What is the one truth Jesus is teaching us through these two statements?

Is Jesus saying that we shouldn't pray out loud? What does it really mean to pray "in secret" (v. 6)?

Day 15

Read Matthew 6:19–34

Jesus has just taught us to pray: "Give us today our daily bread" (v. 11). In other words, "Lord, help us to be content with what we need for today and not worry about tomorrow." He now goes into more detail.

He begins by warning us against the fatal attraction of riches, using three illustrations about two treasures (vv. 19–20), two visions (vv. 21–23), and two masters (v. 24).

Since all earthly things wear out, logically we should invest in what will last: treasures in heaven (vv. 19–20). Jesus has spent the last chapter and half of chapter 6 describing this heavenly treasure: living a life of true righteousness (see Matthew 6:33). With the next metaphor (vv. 21–23), Jesus is saying that if you want an insight into a person's heart, there is no better guide than their attitude towards their possessions. As the eye is the lamp of the body, our attitude to wealth is the barometer of our heart. Just as we saw with performing our righteousness in public, this is one area where we can often fool others, but not God. I can live a materialistic life of stinginess and few would ever know. But God does.

The last picture (v. 24) packs the biggest punch of all. In the end, the choice is black and white: God or possessions. Jesus portrays money as a master with complete control over a person. That is why money is so deceptively powerful, because while people think they are using their money, the reality is that it is using them. This is easy to prove: if I am the master and money is my servant, then I can give it away, but if money is the master, then I cannot. A rich ruler will face this situation later in the gospel (Matthew 19:16ff).

Instead of trusting what will not last, we can trust our Father, not because He will make our life trouble-free, but because He knows our needs (v. 32). It is not wrong to save and invest, but the first priority is to hunger and thirst for righteousness, which is to desire personal holiness in God's sight (Matthew 5:6). This is the point Jesus has been making all along: focus on a life pleasing to Him, and the rest will fall into place (v. 33).

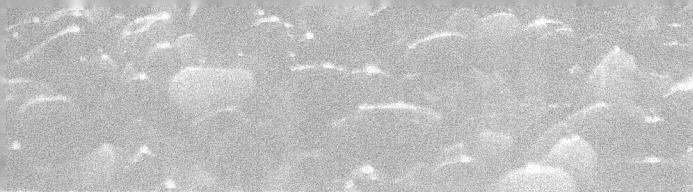

Why do we find
it so hard to be
generous? What
strategies can you
put into place to
ensure that money
doesn't control
your life?

Why do we find it
so hard to trust God
for our material
needs? What point
is Jesus making in
pointing us to the
birds and the flowers
(vv. 26, 28)?

Day 16

Read Matthew 7:1–11

Most people I meet love the Sermon on the Mount and praise its teachings. There are others, however, who find its commands too unrealistic and unattainable. A man once said to me, "I can't do these things and I get really angry at Jesus when He tells me to."

We must remember that the Lord Jesus is a demanding teacher and master, but also a tender pastor and shepherd. **He makes no demand without providing the grace to fulfil it, and gives no command without the promise of forgiveness when we fail.** Every single command in this sermon, if practised, will profoundly deepen our joy and immeasurably improve the quality of our community life as fellow believers.

One of the great temptations for those who seek to keep Jesus' commands is to be judgmental of others. Therefore, Jesus warns us not to judge (v. 1). He does not say that we should not discern or discipline, only that we should not assume a prerogative which belongs to God alone, which is the pronouncement of the final judgment. We should warn the ungodly and assure the saints, but God alone is the judge of each person's life (1 Corinthians 4:4; James 4:12).

On the other hand, we must avoid the opposite danger of being too naive or undiscerning about whom we share the pearls of the gospel. Jesus spoke in parables so that those whose hearts were set against Him would not understand (Matthew 13:13).

All these things can sometimes be difficult for us to do, and so our demanding Lord reveals that He is also the gentle pastor, and reminds us to pray. He bids us simply to ask (v. 7). That is the essence of prayer. We are to keep on asking, seeking, and knocking.

Our relationship with God is not primarily about giving. No, He is the Giver, and what a good Giver He is (v. 11). His good gifts are the very things we have been reading about in this sermon: the power to forgive, to be generous, to be trusting and not anxious, and to be merciful and not judgmental. Yes, the demands can be hard, but with our Lord there is superabundant grace, power, and forgiveness.

How can we fall into the temptation of seeing the splinter in someone else's eye and missing the plank in our own (vv. 3–5)? What steps can we take to ensure we do not behave like this?

I have heard it said, "Don't bring your shopping list of requests to God," yet Jesus bids us to keep on asking Him for things. Can we reconcile these two statements?

Day 17

Read Matthew 7:12–29

Every good preacher concludes with a summary of all He has said, and Jesus does that with the famous Golden Rule (v. 12). This rule concerns the way we relate to others. The guiding principle is: we should treat others in the way we would want others to treat us, for this is what true righteousness is about. Love is at the heart of it.

And now the time has come for the listeners to respond to all that Jesus has taught. But following Him can be tough. He said, "Blessed are those who are persecuted because of righteousness" (Matthew 5:10). This means that those who live righteously will face opposition. So how will we persevere? The Bible gives us two sustaining truths. First come wonderful words of assurance: "For I am convinced that neither death nor life, neither angels nor demons, neither the present nor the future, nor any powers, neither height nor depth, nor anything else in all creation, will be able to separate us from the love of God that is in Christ Jesus our Lord" (Romans 8:38–39). Hand in hand with this are warnings. Jesus, the wise teacher, speaks both. He began His sermon with words of assurance (Matthew 5:3–12), and now He ends it with timely words of warning.

In His final appeal, Jesus reminds us that there are only two choices before us. There are two gates and two roads. There are two ways of living and at the end of each road is either life or destruction. Given all Jesus has said about righteousness, He unsurprisingly warns us that true prophets are discerned not so much by their words as by their behaviour (vv. 15–20).

However, discipleship is not just about confession or mighty works of power. **How does one know he has entered the kingdom of heaven? As Jesus has been teaching all along, only when one's life reflects God's will.** In other words, the proof is in one's obedience to this sermon. Notice that sobering little word, "many" (v. 22). That should drive from our hearts any sense of complacency about living the Christian life. We need His grace and strength.

Jesus concludes with a short parable that summarises all He has said. Building one's house on the rock is a metaphor for hearing and doing Jesus' will (vv. 25–26). On the outside, these two houses look very much the same, but it only takes a storm to reveal what each house is really made of. The storm stands for judgment day, which will separate the two roads, the two prophets, the two confessions, and the two houses.

You see, the hymn was right: "Trust and obey, for there's no other way".

ThinkThrough

Notice how so much of what Jesus says here distinguishes between outward appearance and inward reality. How can we as a church be beguiled by appearances? What does Jesus say is the mark of a true disciple?

"Only a few find it . . . is cut down and thrown into the fire . . . away from me, you evildoers . . . and it fell with a great crash"(vv. 14-27). What and whom is Jesus talking about here? What lessons can we draw from these sobering words?

Day 18

Read Matthew 8:1–17

There were two features of Jesus' ministry: teaching and healing. Matthew 4:23 and 9:35 tell us that Jesus went throughout Galilee, teaching in the synagogues, proclaiming the good news of the kingdom, and healing every disease and illness among the people. These two almost identical verses are like bookends to chapters 5 to 9. In chapters 5, 6, and 7, we are given an example of Jesus' teaching and preaching, and then in chapters 8 and 9 we are given examples of His works of power.

In chapters 8 and 9, Matthew presents nine miracles of Jesus, which display the wide spectrum of His powerful works: people are healed, a storm is stilled, demons cast out, a dead girl is raised, and blind people receive their sight. The nine miracles are arranged in three groups of three (Matthew 8:1–17; 8:23–9:8; 9:18–34) and after each threesome, there is a call to follow Jesus (8:18–22; 9:9–17; 9:36–38).

In Matthew 8:1–17, Jesus displays His power and compassion to individuals belonging to three of the most marginalised groups in Jewish society: a leper (vv. 1–3), a Gentile (vv. 5–13), and a woman (vv. 14–15).

Having the power to heal is one thing, being willing to do so is another. The leper asks, "If you are willing, you can make me clean" (v. 2). He has no doubt about Jesus' power, but he needs assurance of Jesus' willingness. Jesus responds, "I am willing . . . be clean" (v. 3). Similarly, in the next story, a Gentile centurion knows of the authority of Jesus. Indeed, so powerful is the word of Jesus that the centurion believes He can effect a healing simply by speaking—from a distance. Again, Jesus has both the authority and the compassion. Finally, there is the healing of Peter's mother-in-law. All three miracles reveal the power of Jesus' words and the compassion of His heart.

Throughout these chapters we meet the unique authority of Jesus. During His Sermon on the Mount, the crowds are amazed at the authority of His words (Matthew 7:29), and here they stand in awe of the authority of His works. **Jesus still exercises the same authority today. We are invited to personally believe in both His power to teach and transform, and His deep desire to do so.**

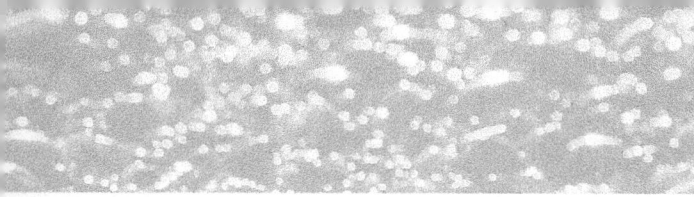

What causes us to doubt the power of Jesus? What causes us to doubt His compassion and willingness to help us?

Look at Matthew 8:10–12. What is Jesus saying about the sort of people who will be with Him in the age to come?

Day 19

Read Matthew 8:18–34

It would be hard to remain unimpressed by Jesus' miracles. For some people, such wonders lead to genuine faith. For others, they engender only superficial allegiance to Jesus, not the kind of costly discipleship He is looking for.

Before Matthew gives us more examples of Jesus' powerful authority, he reminds us of the character of true discipleship. We are given two examples of would-be disciples who must learn that following Jesus means putting Him first (vv. 18–22). Jesus is not introducing any new laws here. He is not saying that homelessness, an itinerant lifestyle, and disregard for one's family are necessary prerequisites for discipleship. Far from it! The Bible states that we have a God-given responsibility to care for our family (see 1 Timothy 5:8). Yet, submitting to the lordship of Jesus relativises all these other relationships (Matthew 10:37). As thousands of missionaries will testify, sometimes the demands of the kingdom will mean leaving family and home.

Jesus has the right to make such exclusive demands because of who He is. Matthew gives us two more breathtaking snapshots of Jesus' unique authority. With a word He calms a violent storm (vv. 23–27). Psalms says that God, and God alone, controls the seas and the storms (Psalm 89:8–9; 135:6–7). Yet here creation submits to the voice of "Immanuel".

Then, on the other side of the lake in Gadarene, a largely Gentile territory, Jesus again demonstrates His total authority over all demonic forces. The demons ask God's Son not to punish them "before the appointed time" (v. 29), that is, before the final day of judgment. Jesus sends them, appropriately, into a herd of unclean animals. Invading the pigs, the demons demonstrate their essentially malevolent character, and immediately destroy the animals. Satan always comes to destroy, while Jesus comes to set free and bring life.

If all creation and all the forces of darkness bow immediately at this man's authoritative word, what should we do? How can we put home, family, career, money, hobbies, or addictions before Him? Now is the day for all to submit to Jesus, "before the appointed time".

Take my life and let it be,
consecrated Lord to thee . . .
Take my will and make it thine,
it shall be no longer mine . . .
—*Francis Havergal*

How can you reconcile being loving and responsible towards your family, and being obedient to Jesus' exclusive demands?

Why do you think the people "pleaded with him to leave" (v. 34) after Jesus cast out the demons? What different responses have you witnessed from people to displays of the power and authority of Jesus?

Day 20

Read Matthew 9:1–17

Good health is a blessing. Medical science has made great progress in improving people's physical health. People are living longer. I heard a forecast recently that we will soon be able to regenerate any part of the body, and so there will not be a Special Olympics after 2030 because there will no longer be anyone with a disability! We will see. Sadly, our personal report card on spiritual health is much grimmer.

When some men bring a paralysed man to Jesus, the Lord's first words are surprising: "Your sins are forgiven" (v. 2). Jesus is telling him—and us—that his greatest sickness is spiritual. Jesus is warning us not to look at the outside. Appearances do not always conform to reality. In His mercy, Jesus gives the man both physical and spiritual healing, for He has authority to heal and to forgive.

Driving home the point that Jesus has come to deal with our greatest need, Matthew then describes the salvation of a hated tax collector (Matthew himself), and the ensuing party with other sinners. In response to the criticisms of the Pharisees, Jesus again teaches about our greatest need, telling them that it is the spiritually sick who are the focus of His ministry.

Jesus' coming means a new day has dawned. Things can never be the same again. His listeners simply cannot relate to God in the ways they did before, through priests, sacrifices, temples, and altars (vv. 16–17). Now everyone must come to God through Jesus. The word "bridegroom"(v. 15) is a reference to the Messiah's coming and His wedding feast (2 Corinthians 11:2; Ephesians 5:23-32; Revelation 19:7, 9; 21:2). By using this term to refer to himself, Jesus is claiming to be the promised Messiah. Those who come to Him will celebrate (vv. 14–15). Joy is the hallmark of the forgiven sinner.

Jesus meets a paralytic and we would have said that his greatest need is to walk again. But we would have been wrong. His greatest need is forgiveness. When we see wars across our world and conflicts in our families, we would say that the greatest need is national peace and mutual reconciliation. Again, we would be wrong. **The greatest need of every nation and every person is to know the Prince of Peace who can forgive their sins.**

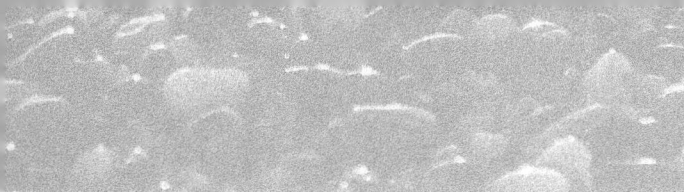

If Jesus came to those who were spiritually sick, why should we still devote time and energy to the physical and temporal needs of people?

What do you find worth celebrating in our knowledge of the Lord Jesus? How can we make our Christian gatherings more celebratory?

Day 21

Read Matthew 9:18–34

It may seem obvious, but the Bible is not about you or me. While the Bible tells us about ourselves and addresses the issues and problems of life, the subject of the Bible is God and how He has saved the world through His Son. The first question one must ask when reading Matthew's gospel is: What does it teach me about Jesus? The second question should then be: What does it teach me about how I should respond to Him?

Matthew now completes his stunning overview of the miracles of Jesus. Here we see Him raising the dead (vv. 18–19, 23–25), healing a woman with a chronic haemorrhage (vv. 20–22), giving sight to the blind (vv. 27–31), and enabling the dumb to speak (vv. 32–33). Each of these people is in torment: a distraught father whose young daughter has died; an unclean woman living in misery for 12 years; two men locked in a world of perpetual darkness; and a man in captivity to Satan, unable to speak. Jesus ends their torment.

What does this teach us about Jesus? He is a man of unparalleled authority. In Genesis 1 God spoke and creation came into being. Here Jesus speaks and His broken creation is made right. More than that, He is a man of compassion whose heart is deeply moved by the brokenness of people's lives.

What does this teach us about our response to Jesus? The people respond in faith: the father knows that if Jesus is there, his dead daughter "will live" (v. 18); the woman knows that if she touches Jesus, "I will be healed" (v. 21); the blind men know He can heal them (v. 28). This is the response Jesus wants from us. Notice the focus is not on the power of the faith of the people, but the power of the One who is the object of their faith.

Jesus is just as powerful today. We do not demand that He answer our prayers in the way we would like, but we know He can. **There is nothing Jesus' powerful word cannot effect, and His compassionate heart is still deeply moved by the brokenness in people's lives.**

What are some of
the wrong notions
that people have
about faith? In light
of this passage, how
would you define
faith?

Why do you think
Jesus sternly warned
the blind men to
keep quiet about
who had restored
their sight (v. 30)?
Why do you think
they ignored Jesus'
command? What
would Jesus have
us do?

Day 22

Read Matthew 9:35–10:15

We have just seen Jesus' loving ministry to a broken world, but the task of announcing the kingdom and calling people into it needs many more workers. Jesus looks at the suffering and bullied crowds, and announces that there is much to do and far too few to do it.

Matthew recorded five collections of Jesus' teachings. The Sermon on the Mount (chapters 5–7) was His first, meant primarily for the disciples. Now He teaches them in His Sermon on the Mission (Matthew 10:5–42).

Jesus first gives them travel instructions. I travel a lot, often for just a few days at a time. For short trips I just take carry-on luggage; I do not want to waste time checking in heavy bags. Jesus tells His disciples to travel light as He sends them out on a short-term mission to the neighbouring towns and villages of Galilee.

This was a limited assignment: they were to go only to Jewish areas (v. 5). The apostle Paul said that the gospel was "first for the Jew" (Romans 1:16). In a little while the floodgates of salvation will open for the Gentiles (see Luke 10:1–17), but here Jesus affirms that, at this stage in God's plan, His covenant people are the focus of His ministry.

These Jews have seen the miracles of Jesus and the disciples and they have the Scriptures, which promised that when the Messiah came He would do the very works that are being performed in front of them (e.g., Isaiah 35:5–6). Given all this evidence, they had no excuse for rejecting the ministry of the apostles.

Those who welcomed Jesus' emissaries received the blessings of peace and salvation. Shaking off dust was a symbolic act of a pious Jew when they left a ceremonially unclean pagan area (v. 14). Therefore, those who rejected Jesus' emissaries found themselves counted among the unclean and, on the final judgment day, outside the kingdom.

Some things are different now. We go to Jews and Gentiles. We often take many bags, for we may stay for years in a particular area proclaiming the kingdom. We will give people who do not know the Scriptures many opportunities to respond (e.g., Acts 19:8–10). Nevertheless, some things remain the same. **There is still an urgent need for people to commit themselves to gospel work. We still make proclamation our first work. The gospel still promises and brings the eternal peace of God.**

As you look at the world around you, what evidence is there of people being harassed and helpless (Matthew 9:36)?

What sort of workers are needed for today's harvest field? How has the Lord gifted and equipped you to serve in this work?

Day 23

Read Matthew 10:16–42

If a missionary society were to have a coat of arms it might have four panels, each with an animal: wolf, sheep, serpent, and dove. These four creatures colourfully portray the character and challenge of the church on mission. Disciples are often weak and vulnerable (sheep) in the midst of a hostile society (wolves), and so they must marry cunning (snake) with guilelessness and innocence (dove).

Jesus is sending out His followers to proclaim the gospel. Knowing that they will meet opposition, He wisely prepares them. Forewarned is forearmed. Our mission of taking the gospel to the world has not changed, nor has the opposition of those who oppose the true God. Yet, whatever the context, we are never alone, for God's Spirit is with us, strengthening us and giving us the boldness to speak (v. 20).

This opposition will come from governing authorities and even our closest relatives (vv. 18, 21). Jesus tells us not to be afraid because, firstly, the gospel just has to be preached; we cannot keep silent (vv. 26–27). Secondly, what is the worst a person can do to us? Destroy our body. How much wiser to fear and serve the One who governs our eternal destiny (v. 28). Nothing will ever happen to us unless our sovereign Father permits it. He loves us deeply and will protect and care for us (vv. 29–31).

Jesus is Lord of all and, therefore, supreme over everything and everyone. Acknowledging, serving, and preaching Him must be our first duty. From time to time there may be conflict between the demands that the world, or even our family, places on us, and the call to follow Christ. At that point the choice that each Christian faces is stark and clear. Yet here is the great paradox: those who make these ultimate sacrifices actually win! They find life, both now and forever (vv. 32–38).

Finally, because disciples are serving Jesus, anyone who receives their ministry is receiving the Son and the Father, and will live forever (vv. 39–42). What a privilege to proclaim the kingdom!

You sometimes hear a person described as a "nominal Christian". There is no such thing. If Jesus is not Lord of all, He is not Lord at all!

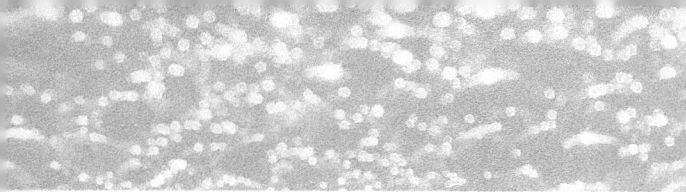

Whom do you fear?
Do you often meet
fearful Christians?
Whom does the
Bible tell us to fear
(v. 28)? How should
this impact our other
fears?

Think about some
situations where you
may be tempted
to compromise
your commitment
to Christ. How
can remembering
Matthew 10 help
us face these
challenges?

Day 24

Read Matthew 11:1–15

Sometimes in the Christian life, things just do not add up. We cannot work out what God is doing. We may find ourselves asking: If God loves me, then why has this happened to me? We can become discouraged and demoralised.

There was a time in the life of John the Baptist when things did not add up, particularly concerning Jesus. In his preaching, John had warned wicked Israel that the Messiah was coming in judgment, and that He would burn up all the ungodly (Matthew 3:12). Yet, it appears that the only one facing death is John himself, languishing in prison (see Matthew 14:1–12). What's more, he has been hearing reports of Jesus' ministry, and while there are wonderful works of mercy, there has been no judgment. What happened to the "winnowing fork" (Matthew 3:12)? John is confused (vv. 2–3).

Jesus reminds John of the words of Isaiah (Isaiah 35:5–6; 61:1), who spoke of the signs and wonders that would mark the coming age of salvation. These are the very deeds that accompany Jesus' ministry. Jesus is the long-awaited Saviour and He is inaugurating the kingdom. There will be judgment in the future, but today is the day of mercy.

Jesus then bears witness to John, the greatest of all the prophets (v. 11). No prophet spoke so clearly about the coming Christ as John did (Matthew 3:1–12; Luke 3:1–18; John 1:6–9; 15–34). Yet even John could not fully comprehend the character and work of Jesus. Only those who live on this side of the cross and resurrection, the "least in the kingdom" (v. 11), you and me, can speak so unambiguously about the Servant King, who came to make atonement for sin, and conquer death once and for all.

God's kingdom has always been powerfully advancing. Throughout history and across the world, people are turning and submitting to the Lord Jesus. Yet, as the kingdom advances, its enemies have always tried to destroy it (v. 12). **These have always been the twin marks of kingdom work: powerful growth and relentless opposition.**

John was confused, and so Jesus took him back to the Scriptures, all of which point to Him (v. 13). That is where we go when we are confused. Until the day we meet the Lord, when we will fully understand, we can trust Him whom we wonderfully meet in the Bible.

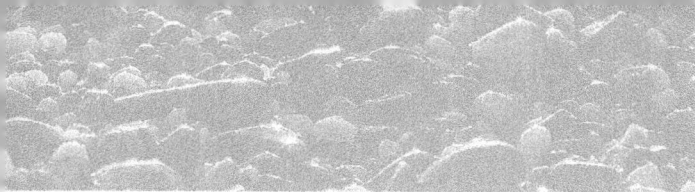

John was confused about both the circumstances of his life and what Jesus was doing. Can you identify with John? Why did Jesus take John to the Bible? Do you think that answered all his questions?

How have you seen the kingdom powerfully advancing in your context? How have you experienced opposition? What comfort can these verses bring?

Day 25

Read Matthew 11:16–30

We are "born again believers". Do you see the paradox in that simple statement? We are born again, which is the Spirit's sovereign work, bringing us to spiritual life. But at the same time, we are also believers. That is, at some point in our life, we chose to put our trust in Christ. It is God's work and our work.

Jesus has just told us of the opposition the kingdom of heaven faces, and now He condemns Israel for their hard-hearted refusal to believe and repent. They are like whinging little children; no matter what you do, they cannot be pleased. John fasts and they call him mad. Jesus feasts and they call Him a glutton (vv. 18–19). Both John and Jesus called the people to repent, yet many rejected and opposed them. In the face of the godly lives of both men (v. 19), and Jesus' extraordinary miracles, still the towns and cities of Galilee have shown a stubborn rebelliousness that outdoes even those infamous twin cities of sin, Sodom and Gomorrah (vv. 23–24). They have made their choice against Jesus. When judgment comes, there can be no excuses. They are fully responsible.

These proud cities will not repent, nor can they repent. Their eyes have been closed to all God is doing in Jesus. But God is sovereign, and it is His will that the little children (v. 25)— that is, the poor in spirit, the meek, and the hungry for righteousness (Matthew 5:1–11)—understand spiritual truths. Jesus always reveals the Father to such people. This is Jesus' sovereign will and power (v. 27).

These words are not meant to dishearten us. On the contrary, this same Jesus invites all of us to "Come" (v. 28). **Anyone who is weighed down by life and guilt can turn in humble dependence to Jesus and find rest in Him.** It is not that following Jesus isn't demanding; indeed, it is the most demanding life of all. Yet the obedience He calls for is exceeded by the grace and strength He provides (v. 30).

We have met today both the sovereign, judging Lord (vv. 20–24), and the gentle, gracious Christ (vv. 25–30). To all who turn to Him, He promises rest, both now in part, and perfectly in the age to come.

Why is Jesus
so strong in His
denunciation of the
Jewish towns and
villages (vv. 20–24)?
Can you think of any
circumstances where
He might say similar
words about the
church?

Would you describe
the people around
you as "weary and
burdened"? How
might you begin to
talk to such people
about the good
news of Jesus?

Day 26

Read Matthew 12:1–14

The Gospels not only describe Jesus' life and ministry as He makes His way to the cross, but also the ever-intensifying confrontation between Him and the Jewish leaders who, eventually, out of hatred put Him to death.

Jesus has already said that He has come to fulfil the law (Matthew 5:17–20), and He has just announced that He gives rest to those who are burdened (Matthew 11:28–30). By contrast, the Pharisees had taken God's wonderful gift of a day of rest and corrupted it, making it a yoke (burden) that inhibited love and goodness.

In this passage, Jesus confronts the Pharisees and demonstrates the true meaning and intention of the Sabbath. The Pharisees prohibited picking grain on the Sabbath because this was considered work ("reaping"). Jesus exposes the Pharisees as the real nit-pickers. He gives two Old Testament examples to demonstrate how the Pharisees misunderstood the purpose of the law.

Firstly, David and his friends satisfied their hunger by eating bread reserved for priests (vv. 3–4; 1 Samuel 21:1–6). Secondly, the priests technically had to "work" on Sabbath to allow the life-giving temple ministry to continue (vv. 5–6; Numbers 28:9–10). In both instances, concession was given in keeping with the spirit of the law, for it is always lawful to save life (Luke 6:9) and to do good even on Sabbath (Matthew 12:12).

Now the Lord Jesus, who fulfils and explains the true intent of the law, has come. As Lord of the Sabbath, He has authority to teach the true purpose of the Sabbath, and part of that is to meet human needs.

Later that day, knowing the Jews are trying to trap Him, Jesus deliberately heals a man whose life has been made miserable by a shrivelled hand. If any day is a good day to show love, surely it is the Sabbath.

In one action, Jesus shows the purpose of the Sabbath. Like all God's commandments, it was given to enrich life, not ruin it. The murderous response of the Pharisees shows both how little they understand the law they have been appointed to teach, and the true character of their hearts.

Again we see the authority of Jesus. He alone has the right to interpret the law of God, for He is the Lord of the Sabbath. He demonstrates that the real goal of the law is love. **However we choose to spend the day of rest, it should be a day filled with**

worshipful delight in God, and in love and service to those around us.

ThinkThrough

Why were the Pharisees so angry at Jesus' behaviour on the Sabbath?

Can you think of instances where we might forget that God desires mercy and not sacrifice?

Day 27

Read Matthew 12:15–37

On the T-shirt of a young man who walked by me was this announcement: "Bad Is Good." Perhaps he wasn't expressing his true philosophy of life, but few things demonstrate the corruption of the human race better than the fact that we justify evil with the defence that it is good.

In this next passage, Jesus continues to bring life and healing to the sick and demon-possessed (v. 15, 22), just as Isaiah had prophesied (Isaiah 42:1–4). It therefore beggars belief that the Pharisees called this compassionate and powerful ministry of Jesus "demonic" (see v. 24).

It would be ridiculous to think that Satan, who seeks to maim and destroy, would empower a man to heal and restore. Jesus exposes the absurdity of their assertion that He is in league with Beelzebub, or Satan. Why would any general kill his own men? Why would a king destroy his own kingdom (vv. 25–27)? No, Jesus' defeat of the forces of darkness unquestionably establishes Him as the true King, who has come to establish His kingdom of peace and justice (vv. 28–29).

The Pharisees had no excuse for their outrageous claim. Jesus' miracles spoke for themselves. It wasn't that the Pharisees could not believe—they would not believe. They deliberately and repeatedly spurned the Spirit-empowered ministry of Jesus. These men were not sincere seekers of the truth. Their questions did not reflect genuine doubt. Theirs was a resolute, steadfast refusal to believe. They knew, deep down, that only God's Spirit could empower such works. Therefore, to then wilfully call the Spirit's work "devilish" is nothing short of an unforgivable blasphemy (see vv. 31–32). Since they totally rejected Jesus, there exists no other way for them to come to God (John 14:6).

Why does anyone treat Jesus with such contempt? Ultimately, it is a matter of the heart (vv. 33–37). Similarly, a life of love to God and others, characterised by gracious and caring words, reflects a heart made right by God's Spirit. **Hearts are never silent; what hides in the heart will find its way to the lips.** Then on judgment day, words spoken, even careless ones (like Bad Is Good), which either honour or despise the Son, will testify to the state of the heart, and therefore God will use them to judge each person's heart (or character).

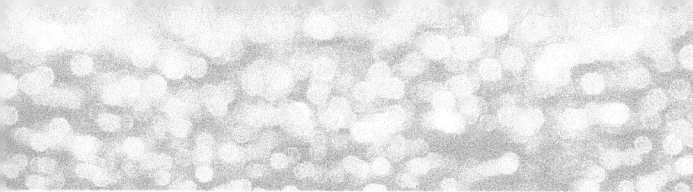

What would you say to a Christian who was anxious that he or she had committed the unforgivable sin?

The Bible has a lot to say about the power of "words" (e.g., Proverbs 10:8–21; Ephesians 5:4–7; James 3:1–12). Why does the Bible have so much to say about words? What is the relationship between salvation and the words we speak?

Day 28

Read Matthew 12:38–50

How often has someone said, "I would believe in God if He would just give me a sign"? Sometimes this can be a genuine request, and sometimes God graciously answers the prayer. However, there is nothing genuine about the request of the scribes and Pharisees for a sign from Jesus. They have already seen many miracles by Jesus (Matthew 11:20–23). What more do they need? Besides, Jesus has just made it clear that they have already made up their minds about Him (Matthew 12:22–32), and more displays of His divine power would not make any difference.

Echoing the earlier preaching of John the Baptist (Matthew 3:1–12), Jesus condemns not just the leaders of the Jews but the Jewish people themselves as a "wicked and adulterous generation" (v. 39). He will one day give them a sign, the greatest sign of all: His resurrection from the dead. Jesus calls this "the sign of the prophet Jonah"—not just because Jonah spent three days in "the heart of the earth", but because it was pagans who responded to his preaching, just like the pagan Queen of Sheba recognised in Solomon divine wisdom (vv. 39–42; see 1 Kings 10:1–9). After Jesus' resurrection, Gentiles will again respond to the gospel of the risen Christ. Yet, as a nation under their religious authorities, the wilfully blind Jews refuse to recognise the One in their midst who is greater than either Jonah or Solomon.

The next short parable (vv. 43–45) warns of the danger of not responding to Jesus. There is no neutral position. To have heard the gospel and seen evidence of God's power in people's lives (like the Jews of Jesus' day), and yet not respond with wholehearted commitment, is to leave yourself in a worse spiritual condition than before.

What, then, is the right response to Jesus? Our Lord repeats what He said at the end of the Sermon on the Mount: it is to do the will of the Father (v. 50; cf. Matthew 7:24). **Those who obey the Lord are more than just His disciples; they are His brothers and sisters. What an unspeakable privilege!** Jesus isn't demeaning His earthly family; He is exalting His disciples. The holy transcendent God is our heavenly Father, and the awesome, divine Lord of heaven and earth is more intimately related to us than even our earthly family.

When people ask God for a sign, what do you think they are looking for? Is it ever right to ask for a sign? When do you think it is wrong?

"God only has children, not grandchildren." In the light of what Jesus says here about His family, what does that popular saying mean? How can you be sure that you have a relationship with the Lord Jesus?

Day 29

wonder if the disciples were sometimes confused about all that was happening. On the one hand, vast crowds were flocking to hear Jesus and see His signs, while on the other hand, opposition was becoming more intense. People seemed to be responding to Jesus in such different ways. This is true even today. Why are people's responses to Jesus so varied?

Because of opposition from the Jews, from here on Jesus would teach in parables. In this chapter, Matthew gives us a sample of Jesus' parables about the kingdom of heaven. The first parable addresses the question of the different responses to His preaching (vv. 18–23).

Jesus describes preaching God's Word as being like a farmer sowing seeds. People's hearts are like the different kinds of ground the seed falls upon. You can put a name to each of these people. Mary hears the Word, and immediately a voice whispers, "This isn't for you," and she walks away (v. 19). Tony enthusiastically hears and responds, but then he gives up as family and friends ridicule him (vv. 20–21). John hears the Word, but louder voices like the call of career and wealth drown it out (v. 22). Beth hears the Word, trusts Jesus, and lives a life of joyful obedience that blesses many (v. 23). These are four different "soils" which reflect four different responses to God's Word.

Why did Jesus speak in parables? In part, it was to help people understand spiritual truths. Stories aid understanding. Yet Jesus also told parables so that some would not understand (vv. 10–12). We have just seen that some Jewish people have already made up their minds against Jesus (Matthew 9:34; 12:14, 24). Despite the undeniable evidence, they have hardened their hearts. They *will* not understand, so now God has made it that they cannot understand (vv. 13–17). There is a point where God's patience with steadfast unbelief runs out.

Through parables, Jesus is telling "the secrets of the kingdom" (v. 11). By definition a secret is not known to everyone. **Those who have closed their ears do not hear. Those with open ears hear the secret and pass it on.** Such people, says Jesus, are incredibly blessed (v. 16). Let us thank God for giving us His Word, and let us resolve to keep our hearts receptive to it.

Think of people you know who have not responded to Jesus. Can you identify them as one of the "soils" that Jesus describes here? How would you continue to minister to each of these different kinds of people?

There is a sober warning in these verses against hardening our hearts. How can we ensure that our hearts remain tender and responsive to God's Word? How can we pray for those who appear to have closed their minds to the good news?

Day 30

Read Matthew 13:24–43

The popular Australian singer and songwriter, Paul Kelly, has a song that goes, "From little things big things grow". That is a good summary of the main point of the next few parables (vv. 24–30, 31–32, 33–34). Jesus the King has come, and while crowds are attracted to Him, relatively few obey His word to leave everything and follow Him. Today in much of the world, Christians are a tiny, often voiceless minority. Indeed, in some places the church appears to be in retreat. Why is God's kingdom apparently so small? Why doesn't God do something? These parables are Jesus' answer.

The parable of the wheat and the weeds (vv. 24–30, 37–43) again addresses a question which may have been troubling the disciples: Why are so many rejecting Jesus? The apostle Paul says that Satan "has blinded the minds of unbelievers, so that they cannot see the light of the gospel that displays the glory of Christ" (2 Corinthians 4:4). Jesus identifies the devil as the one who has turned people away from God. Indeed, unbelievers are "the people of the evil one" (v. 38). For the present, believer and unbeliever live side-by-side in this world. A day of final judgment is approaching though, when God will act against evil and finally separate the wheat from the weeds.

The parables of the mustard seed (vv. 31–32) and the yeast (vv. 33–35) address the question of why God's kingdom—that is, Jesus' rule over the hearts of people—seems so small. Jesus' answer is that appearances are deceiving. Certainly the beginnings of the kingdom were modest, but it will grow and grow until it is "a great multitude that no one could count" (Revelation 7:9). Its growth will often be quiet and indiscernible, yet just like yeast silently makes its way through the whole loaf, the gospel "is bearing fruit and growing throughout the whole world" (Colossians 1:6).

Do not be discouraged; God is in control. His kingdom is growing, even in your part of the world. Do not lose heart; the day is coming when all evil will finally be banished, and "the righteous will shine like the sun in the kingdom of their Father" (v. 43).

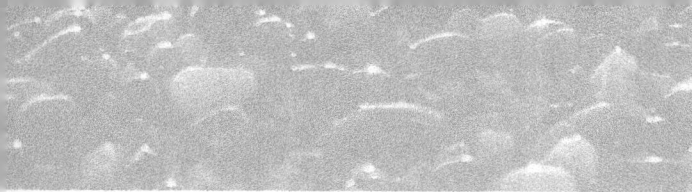

ThinkThrough

Do you sometimes become discouraged by the "smallness" of the kingdom? What kinds of things discourage you? How can Jesus' words here help when we feel this way?

Why do you think we hear so little in many churches about the final judgment, when Jesus spoke about it so often? What comfort can teaching about the final judgment bring to Christians?

Day 31

Read Matthew 13:44–53

Author C . S. Lewis described his coming to faith in the Lord Jesus with these words: "I was now approaching the source from which those arrows of joy which had been shot at me ever since childhood . . . union with God's nature is bliss and separation from it is horror." That is a good summary of the main points of our Lord's next three parables.

Jesus describes finding the kingdom as being like stumbling across a treasure in a field (v. 44) or a priceless pearl (v. 45). Or, in today's terms, it is like being informed that you have a long-lost aunt in England who has left you a billion dollars! What do you do? After ascertaining the truth of the matter, you will spend all your savings on a flight to London to claim your inheritance. Knowing Jesus and His salvation is worth more than anything in the world, and it is worth any sacrifice to obtain it. Finding the kingdom involves sacrifice, but so wonderful is the treasure that one hardly notices the cost because of the "arrows of joy".

The other side of the coin is the horror of not knowing Christ. How unimaginable that someone could discover this treasure and then decide that it is not worth the trouble of buying the field to lay claim to it (v. 44). In the parable of the net (vv. 47–50), Jesus again propels us forward to the last judgment. While He describes many varieties of fish within the gospel net, there are really only two kinds: good fish, who respond to the gospel, are kept forever; and the bad ones, who do not respond, are thrown away. There are consequences to our decisions.

Over the last four days, we have heard Jesus preach the good news of the kingdom. By God's grace, we have been given understanding of these wonderful, eternal truths. How then should we respond?

Jesus' final parable is about a teacher who shares his wealth of knowledge (v. 52). We should now understand that while we have an Old Testament ("old treasures") and a New Testament ("new treasures"), they proclaim one message: the salvation found in Jesus, the promised Messiah. **This good news is not a treasure we can keep to ourselves. The rich share their wealth with the poor. We who have been taught must now be teachers of others.**

ThinkThrough

Think back to when you first discovered the wonder of the gospel. What was it about knowing Christ that filled you with joy? How can we ensure that nothing robs us of this joy?

"He went and sold all he had." What does a "costless Christianity" look like? How can the Christian life be simultaneously a life of sacrifice and joy?

Day 32

Read Matthew 13:54–14:12

I n His missionary sermon (Matthew 10), Jesus warned His disciples of rejection and persecution on two fronts: "you will be brought before governors and kings" (Matthew 10:18), and your own family will oppose you (Matthew 10:21). As Matthew records the mounting opposition against Jesus, we see both domestic and political aspects.

I was born and raised in Liverpool, England. I remember, as a young boy, sitting on my father's shoulders as the crowds lined the streets to welcome back our world-conquering heroes, The Beatles. We were proud that four sons of our city had achieved such success.

It is remarkable, then, that while Jesus was being acclaimed everywhere else, people in His hometown of Nazareth were so cynical and unbelieving (vv. 53–58). Perhaps they were jealous that such an "ordinary" man should find such fame? Perhaps they were offended that He, one of them, should be telling them how to live? Perhaps they were angry that He wasn't using His powers more for the benefit of His hometown? Whatever the reason, they refuse to believe in Him and dismiss Him as unworthy of honour. Only where there is faith will Jesus bring the blessings of salvation.

Matthew deliberately places the story of John the Baptist's death next to his account of the rejection of Jesus. John had publicly condemned Herod for his incestuous marriage to the wife of his half-brother. Israel's faithful prophets called Israel to return to the Lord by trusting Him and turning away from evil. Many paid the ultimate price for their faithful preaching. John the Baptist stands in this noble tradition: boldly preaching, even at the cost of his own life. Of course, this prepares us for the ultimate sacrifice of the One who is greater than John.

These two stories remind us that since the gospel is a confronting message, those who preach this gospel may face the same angry response as Jesus and John. Jesus was both misunderstood and dishonoured. John and Jesus were killed because they preached the gospel of God faithfully and without compromise. While the ministries of John and Jesus were unique, the response to their preaching is not. **All who faithfully proclaim God's Word will meet faith and repentance, but also unbelief, misunderstanding, and opposition.** This is Jesus' call to all who proclaim Him: a great cost but a glorious reward.

Why are close family
and friends often
difficult to reach with
the gospel? How
can we appropriately
share our faith with
them?

How does the
murder of John the
Baptist prepare us
for what will happen
to Jesus?

Day 33

Read Matthew 14:13–36

Language keeps changing, which is natural, but sometimes in the evolution of language, the meaning of words is devalued. One example is "unique". Today you hear people say, "It was quite unique", or "He is very unique". "Unique" means "one of a kind". Something cannot be "quite" or "very" one of a kind. Someone either stands alone, with no rivals, or he does not. Today we see the uniqueness of Jesus, and Matthew's description renders absurd any attempt to liken the Lord Jesus to any other man or woman.

This passage is bracketed by references to the unrelenting pressure of the crowds upon Jesus (vv. 13, 35). It was exhausting for Him, and so Matthew records two occasions when He went away by himself to pray (vv. 13, 23).

In the first instance, the crowds followed Him. There were 5,000 men and so, with women and children, around 15,000 to 20,000 people (v. 21). Matthew contrasts this vast crowd with the paltry amount of food: just five loaves and two fish. Jesus then did what only God does, and miraculously created food and fed them all. Twelve is the biblical number for completion (12 disciples, 12 tribes), so the fact that there are 12 baskets of leftovers implies that there was enough food that day to feed all of God's people (v. 20). This Jesus is unique.

Again, Jesus retreated to pray (v. 23). During the night, He came to the disciples, whose ship was struggling in a storm (vv. 22–24). He walked upon the water and, in response to their terror-filled cry, announced, "It is I" (v. 27)—or literally, "I am"—the very words Moses heard God speak at the burning bush. This is Yahweh in their midst.

How should we respond to this Jesus? Matthew regularly presents Peter as the spokesman for the 12 disciples (e.g., Matthew 15:15; 16:16; 17:4, 24; 18:21; 19:27). Peter trusts in Jesus and comes to Him as invited, but then takes his eyes off the Lord and focuses on the crisis around him, and begins to sink (vv. 28–30). We can all identify with Peter: periods of great faith followed by doubt and despair.

There can be only one response to the Jesus we have met today: worship and confession, "Truly, you are the Son of God" (v. 33). **This Jesus is unique. Keep your eyes fixed on Him.**

How do we see in this passage both the humanity and the divinity of Jesus?

Why does Peter's faith in Jesus begin to falter (vv. 28–31)? Why does Jesus rebuke Peter for his "little faith"? What lessons do you think Matthew wants us to draw from this remarkable episode?

Day 34

Read Matthew 15:1–20

You may be surprised that the scribes and Pharisees make such a fuss here about the disciples not washing their hands before a meal (v. 2). Today, we might make such a demand of little children, but not adults. So why is there such a fuss?

We need to remember that for the Jewish leaders, the issue here was not one of personal hygiene, but the deeper problem of religious or ceremonial purity. They were right to believe that people need to be clean to enter God's presence, but they were gravely mistaken to think the real pollution was on the outside.

Indeed, that is the essential problem with hypocrisy. It focuses on externals and neglects the heart. The religious leaders had invented many extra laws, ostensibly to keep the people pure, but these laws often had the opposite effect; they actually served to make them selfish.

For example, in "adding" to the command to honour one's parents, they actually subtracted from it (vv. 4–6). This command enjoins upon children a lifelong obligation to love and care for their parents (Exodus 20:12; 21:17). However, the religious lawyers had invented a tradition called "devoted to God" (v. 5). An adult son could now say to his needy parent, "I would love to help pay for your medical bills, but I have just dedicated all my savings to the Lord's service" (see Mark 7:11–12). This provided a loophole for Jews to shirk their responsibility towards their needy parents. Jesus regularly exposed this selfishness masquerading as piety.

Jesus then goes to the *heart* of the issue, and that is the polluted human heart (vv. 10–11). At the core of every human being, a contaminated spring gushes forth, poisoning our personality, relationships, attitudes, desires, and actions. That is the great moral and spiritual pollutant, not unwashed hands or different kinds of food and drink (vv. 16–20). **The problem is on the inside, and that is where the solution must be found. We need a new heart.**

Jesus not only diagnosed the basic human problem, but also went on to deal with it. On the cross, He cleansed us from our sins and brought lasting purification. Then, by His Spirit, He gave His people a new heart with new motivations, attitudes, and desires (Deuteronomy 30:6; Ezekiel 36:26–27).

So much of human religion deals with externals. Can you think of examples? What makes the Christian faith a "religion of the heart"?

Can we make excuses for not "honouring our father and our mother"? What obligations do you think that you have to your parents to love them as God intends?

Day 35

Read Matthew 15:21–39

"am not ashamed of the gospel, because it is the power of God that brings salvation to everyone who believes: first to the Jew, then to the Gentile" (Romans 1:16). This is Paul's important summary of God's salvation plan. Understanding God's timetable helps us to make sense of a passage of Scripture which troubles some people.

Jesus has already explicitly commanded His disciples to preach to Jews and not Gentiles (Matthew 10:5–6). This does not mean God has no desire to save Gentiles. He has already foreshadowed their salvation (Matthew 1; 2; 8:10–12) and very soon Jesus will send the apostles out with a clear command to go to all nations (Matthew 28:19–20). In the meantime, His ministry is mainly directed towards God's covenant people, Israel.

In this passage, Jesus gives us a foretaste of the day when all nations will enjoy the full blessings of salvation. He travels to the Gentile region of Tyre and Sidon and meets a woman whose daughter is demon-possessed. This is Gentile territory and He is found ministering to them as well, but first, He reminds the people of God's timetable.

While the expression "dog" is a harsh one (v. 26), the woman seems to discern that Jesus will grant her request. She is a remarkable woman. Her reply to Jesus (v. 27) is full of wit, wisdom, and faith; Jesus acknowledges this. Indeed, she is the second person in the gospel that Jesus has verbally commended for great faith—and both are Gentiles (cf. Matthew 8:10).

In what is almost a rerun of the feeding of the 5,000, Matthew records Jesus miraculously feeding a crowd of 4,000 men (plus women and children) who are predominantly Gentiles.

Why would Matthew record two such similar events? He has already established Jesus' divine credentials. Surely, he wants us to see that God intends Gentiles to receive the very same salvation blessings that Jesus pours out on Jews.

God's purpose has not changed. The gospel is for both Jews and Gentiles.
Jews must believe in Christ as much as pagan Gentiles, thus we have a special obligation to bring to them the good news of Jesus, who fulfilled all their longings for a Saviour and Messiah.

ThinkThrough

It has been said that Jesus spoke these harsh words to the woman "with a twinkle in His eye". Do you think that might be right? Why was the woman not deterred by Jesus' words?

Given that we have a special obligation to bring the gospel to the Jews, how should this affect your church's mission programme?

Day 36

Read Matthew 16:1–16

If you ask people, "Who is Jesus?", you will receive a variety of responses. I heard someone say, "He was a pretty good bloke." For him, Jesus was a good man and nothing more. Others may say that He was a great moral teacher. Some sceptics even question whether Jesus of Nazareth ever existed.

Matthew 16 is one of the high points of the gospel. From Matthew 1 onwards, the reader has implicitly been asked, "Who is Jesus?" God has spoken (Matthew 3:17) and so have the demons (Matthew 8:29), but what of those who have seen and heard Him?

Jesus has just returned from ministering to Gentiles, who then "praised the God of Israel" (Matthew 15:31). Once more the hostile Jewish leaders approach and try to trap Him by asking for a sign (see Matthew 12:38).

What a contrast! Gentiles believe and rejoice, while Jewish leaders, who have witnessed the same signs, harden their hearts. Remember Jesus' words, "I praise you, Father . . . because you have hidden these things from the wise and learned, and revealed them to little children" (Matthew 11:25). Jesus refuses to pander to their unbelieving demands.

Amazingly, even the disciples do not seem to have fully grasped who Jesus is. Despite witnessing the miracles of the bread and fish on two different occasions (Matthew 14:13–21; 15:29–38), they have not yet understood that they do not need to be anxious, but can trust Jesus to meet their needs (vv. 8–11).

It is then, that Jesus asks them, point blank, who they think He is (v. 15). Once again, Peter steps up as their leader and spokesman and makes the great confession: "You are the Messiah, the Son of the living God" (v. 16). **Jesus is both the promised Messiah who has come to save His people, and God's only Son.** We will later see that there is still much for Peter to understand about Jesus, but his confession displays great spiritual insight.

Peter's confession is impressive and Matthew wants the same confession to be on our lips. But confessing Christ means more than words. It is so important that we give the right answer to the most important question of all, "Who is Jesus?" It is equally important that the confession of our lips be a reflection of the faith in our hearts.

What answers do
your friends and
neighbours give to
the question, "Who
is Jesus?"

If someone really
believes that Jesus is
the Christ and God's
Son, how should
that impact how they
live?

Day 37

Read Matthew 16:17–20

Peter has just spoken and made the great confession about Jesus (v. 16). Jesus now speaks and makes His confession about Peter. Sin has blinded people's spiritual eyes and so God himself needs to enlighten their understanding so that they can see Jesus (cf. Matthew 11:25–27). Ultimately, it is God who has enabled Peter—and you and me—to confess Jesus (v. 17).

There are a couple of views regarding Jesus' confession and one of them is that He now explains to "Peter" why He gave him that name. "Peter" is the masculine form of the Greek word for "rock". It is as if Jesus is saying, "You are 'Rocky' and on this rock I will build my church". It is a play on words, as if God was to say to me, "You are Mike, and through this mike I will broadcast my gospel". Jesus is announcing that Peter's ministry will be foundational to the building of the church.

That is exactly what we find in the book of Acts. After Jesus has ascended, it is Peter who assumes the leadership role in God's building of the church. It is Peter who speaks at Pentecost when the Spirit comes in power on those Jews who believed (Acts 2:1–41), and then preaches to Cornelius and the Spirit comes upon the Gentiles (Acts 10:44–48).

Peter also stands in the Gospels as first among equals. Paul wrote that the church is "built on the foundation of the apostles and prophets, with Christ Jesus himself as the chief cornerstone" (Ephesians 2:20). It was through these men, under Peter's leadership, and their apostolic teaching, that God builds His church, which will never die.

Finally, Jesus makes a remarkable promise to Peter: "I will give you the keys of the kingdom of heaven" (v. 19).

If you have the keys to a house, you can grant entry to some and refuse others. That is what Jesus means by "bind" and "loose" (v. 19). As Peter and the apostles—and, indeed, all who preach this apostolic gospel—announce the good news to people, those who believe are loosed or released from their sins. Those who do not believe are kept outside the kingdom.

If I lose my keys, people cannot enter my house. Or, if I change the key's shape, then the door remains shut. **It is an awesome responsibility and privilege to preach this unchanging, life-saving gospel.**

When God opened
your eyes to
see Jesus and
understand who
He is, how did that
experience impact
your life?

What would you
say is the "apostolic
gospel"? How
can this gospel be
distorted and what
are the ramifications
of this happening?

Day 38

Read Matthew 16:21–28

Jesus now enters the next phase of His ministry: "From that time on . . ." (v. 21). His approaching death will now dominate His teaching.

Peter, speaking for all the disciples, has boldly confessed that Jesus is the long-awaited anointed King. He was right to recognise Jesus as Messiah, but profoundly wrong in his understanding of the nature of Jesus' messiahship. Jesus has come to save not through force of arms, but through arms outstretched in death.

Jesus explicitly teaches the disciples that He must die and rise again (v. 21). This radical proclamation of the purpose of His ministry utterly confounds Peter. Jesus sees behind Peter's rebuke the malevolent hand of Satan, seeking yet again (v. 23; cf. Matthew 4:1–11) to derail His efforts in fulfilling the work God has ordained for Him. Peter, the "rock" on which Jesus will build His church, has become a rock of stumbling.

In one sense, Jesus' death on a cross will not be an isolated event. **Any and every disciple must be prepared to face that same eventuality: to give up all for God's sake.** The command to deny ourselves (v. 24) must not be reduced to something as trivial as a decision not to buy another pair of shoes, or even extend the house. It is to renounce control over one's own life. Throughout history, thousands of Christians have carried a cross to their own Calvary. Martyrs like Jim Elliot, an American missionary who died at the hands of Huaorani Indians in Ecuador on 8 January 1956, famously wrote, "He is no fool who gives what he cannot keep to gain what he cannot lose."

In verse 27, the Lord Jesus underlines the seriousness of the life-and-death decision every disciple must face by reminding us that one day, we will answer to Jesus himself for these decisions. Until that day, when He establishes His kingdom on earth, Jesus' authority and kingly rule will be displayed in His church, especially after Pentecost, as many of His disciples will witness and experience it (v. 28).

The church needs to regularly hear these confronting words from its Lord (v. 27). In the twenty-first century, many Christians face loss and death on a daily basis because of their love for Jesus. On the other hand, many others who surrender to a costless Christianity, indistinguishable in attitude and behaviour from the unbelieving world, need to heed His warning.

What does it mean
in practical terms
for you to "deny
yourself" (v. 24)?

Jesus promises a
reward to faithful
disciples (v. 27).
What might this
reward be? Should
the prospect of a
heavenly reward
affect how we
live now?

Day 39

Read Matthew 17:1–13

There are few passages in the New Testament more awe-inspiring than the transfiguration, literally the "metamorphosis", of Jesus. Jesus had taken Peter, James, and John up a mountain. In the Bible, momentous revelations often take place on mountains: God gave the law to Moses on a mountain (Exodus 19:1–3); Jesus gave the new interpretation of the law on a mountain (Matthew 5:1); the Great Commission was given on a mountain (Matthew 28:16).

Before their eyes, Jesus' form was changed. This is Jesus in His divine glory. Even after His resurrection, before His ascension, the disciples never saw Jesus like this. The one overwhelming impression and sensation they receive is of light: His face and clothes shone. This was not a light that was shining on Him; it was part of His essence. He was the source of the light, and those around Him shielded themselves from the stark glow of the One who is the light of the world.

Then Moses the great lawgiver and Elijah the great prophet appeared before them. Notice the great significance of those five men who are gathered around Jesus. On one side are Moses and Elijah, who symbolise the law and the prophets, the Old Testament. On the other side are the apostles who symbolise the New Testament. They are all focused on Jesus and listening to Him. All of the Old Testament points forward to Jesus and His salvation. The New Testament reveals the fulfilment of God's promises, and explains how His saved people should live. Jesus is the centre of the whole Bible. It has been said that the Old Testament and the New Testament sing duet, but the New Testament carries the melody, and that melody is Jesus.

"This is my Son . . . Listen to him!" (v. 5). This is God's message to the whole world. **Nothing we do can be more important than spending time listening to Jesus.** Matthew's final words are: "When they looked up they saw no one except Jesus" (v. 8). Only Jesus was transfigured. Only Jesus was honoured by God. Only the word of Jesus is to be listened to and obeyed by everyone.

Reflect on verses
6 to 7. What do they
teach us about how
we should respond
to the Lord Jesus?

How important is
listening to Jesus
in your life? What
changes do you
think are needed in
your life to give the
word of Jesus more
prominence?

Day 40

Read Matthew 17:14–27

From the mountain, we now move to the valley. After seeing the transfigured glory of the Lord Jesus, we now see the weakness of the disciples.

Jesus has already given the disciples authority over demons (Matthew 10:1, 8), and they have done mighty works in His name. Now they confront a young boy with a demon that expresses its oppression by causing seizures. There is nothing in this boy's condition that the disciples have not seen before, yet they cannot heal him. The difference is not in the condition of the boy, but in the hearts of the disciples. Since they know God's power over such demonic forces, their failure is inexcusable.

Jesus' disappointment and frustration with His disciples is evident. He rebukes them for their "little faith". We see here two kinds of "little faith". The first is not really faith at all (v. 17): it is faith in word only. The disciples had forgotten all they had experienced of Jesus' ministry and had stopped looking to God. Their faith seems as shallow as the unbelieving society around them.

The second is a faith that Jesus commends. This faith, like a mustard seed, will see mountains move, because this kind of faith trusts in the power and purposes of God (vv. 20–21). **The issue with faith is not how much you have, but where you place it.** It is a big God, more than big faith, which moves mountains.

Jesus again reminds His followers of His impending death, which will mean the end of the old age (v. 22). The temple, God's symbolic dwelling place, was the central institution of that age. As God's Son, Jesus is not subject to requirements like paying a tax for the temple's upkeep (vv. 25–26). Yet He continues to pay it so that He will not cause unnecessary offence. The miraculous provision of the coin demonstrates God's approval of His behaviour (v. 27).

Sometimes you hear people say, "If you had more faith . . ." That can make us look inward and attempt to drum up more faith. No, look more to God. Remind yourself of the God of Matthew's gospel. He is the One who is big! He is the One who is willing and able. He is the mountain mover.

Why does Jesus liken the disciples to their unbelieving generation? Why do you think they have stopped believing in the power of God?

What are the characteristics of "mustard seed faith" (v. 20)? Why do you think Jesus commends this kind of "little faith"?

Day 41

Read Matthew 18:1–14

A friend of mine began to attend our church about 15 years ago. She had no church background, and simply walked into our inner-city church. The church was full of people: professionals as well as the poor and unemployed, families and singles, students and retirees, and those from many different cultures. Yet for all its diversity and its imperfections, my friend was profoundly impressed by the church. "You people go on and on about love", she said. She is still an active member of this remarkable community.

We have seen that Jesus came to bring in a new order, and to gather around himself a new community. This chapter describes the character of this new community.

The disciples continue to display their worldliness by seeking greatness. Jesus takes a child and gives them—and us—a symbol of true greatness in God's eyes. His focus here is not about children being saved because of their simple faith and innocence. Rather, in Jesus' world, a child had no status; they were the least. Jesus described His disciples in similar terms earlier: they are the poor, the meek, the hungry and thirsty (Matthew 5:1–12). They imitate Jesus himself, who assumed a similar position in becoming a slave for us (Philippians 2:1–11).

These children, Jesus' people, are so precious to Him that He warns, in the strongest terms, anyone who causes them serious spiritual harm: better that such a person die first than face God's eternal wrath for ruining one of His beloved children (vv. 6–9).

Rather than cause such a little one to go astray, a true disciple mirrors the love the Father has for them (vv. 10–14). In Ezekiel 34, God castigates Israel's spiritual leaders for their failure to strengthen the weak, heal the sick, bandage the wounded, and bring back the strays. God then promises to restore them himself. The implication is that we should reflect the Father's love in our care for the weak.

This is the mark of the new community of God's people. **They don't just talk about love, but practise it, especially in their care of those most in need.**

ThinkThrough

What does it mean practically to see oneself as having the status of a child?

If we are not meant to take Jesus' words in verses 8 to 9 literally, then how are we to interpret and apply our Lord's warning in these verses?

Day 42

Read Matthew 18:15–35

How do we pastorally care for those who are spiritually straying? Jesus instructs us on how to restore someone who has sinned (vv. 15–20,) and then teaches us about the importance of forgiving anyone who sins against us.

In order to demonstrate that our forgiveness should be as unlimited as God's forgiveness to us (vv. 21–22), Jesus tells a parable about a servant who owes his king an incredible debt of 10,000 talents, which would be equivalent to about 200,000 years' wages. In other words, it is an infinite debt, just as our debt of sin against God is infinite. Then, out of deep compassion, the king freely cancels the debt.

Salvation is all of grace; there is nothing anyone can do to earn it. Yet, as Jesus has repeatedly warned, while God does not set any conditions on sinners receiving His forgiveness, He does expect those forgiven to now live lives of faithful obedience. Salt must be tasty. Light must shine. A good tree will bear good fruit. **Forgiven sinners must forgive those who come to them for forgiveness.**

The forgiven servant refuses forgiveness to someone who, in comparison to his debt to the king, owes him a tiny sum. His hard-heartedness defies belief.

This man made two mistakes: he forgot the amazing grace of God, and he forgot there would be a day of judgment. In the parable, he stands before his king a second time, who now hands him over to the jailers (or literally, "torturers") "until he should pay back all he owed" (v. 34)—his punishment will last as long as the repayment of his debt takes. Since it is impossible to repay such a huge amount, his punishment will last for all eternity. As Jesus said, "Not everyone who says to me, 'Lord, Lord' will enter the kingdom of heaven, but only the one who does the will of my Father who is in heaven" (Matthew 7:21).

God's will is that we forgive one another, and Jesus' disciples hunger and thirst to do His will. This parable asks us two questions. Do we appreciate the cross, the amazing grace of God's free forgiveness? Do we anticipate the coming judgment? Gratitude for grace and fearful obedience will keep us persevering.

What is your
experience of the
amazing grace of
God?

Forgiving someone
who has wronged
us and hurt us can
be very difficult.
How in practical
terms, can we reach
a point of genuine
forgiveness?

Day 43

Read Matthew 19:1–12

Having spent most of His time ministering in Galilee, Jesus now moves south into Judea. This journey will culminate in His death, as the hostility of the Jewish leaders intensifies. Here they test Him with the thorny question of divorce. Unlike today, when either the husband or wife can initiate divorce proceedings, in ancient Israel a man could simply terminate a marriage, often leaving the wife destitute.

Jesus responds by taking them back to Genesis 2 and God's original plan for marriage. **From the beginning, marriage was to be a lifelong, exclusive relationship between a man and a woman. This is still the abiding will of God.**

Moses, knowing human sinfulness and weakness, permitted divorce (Deuteronomy 24:1–4). Some interpreted this concession strictly, allowing divorce only for serious sexual misconduct, but the majority had broadened the concession so that a man could end a marriage on almost any whim (v. 3). However, Jesus says that this concession was in no way intended to undermine God's perfect will for marriage (vv. 4–8). While unfaithfulness breaks the marriage bond and is grounds for divorce (v. 9)—although, as Jesus has just pointed out, even there we should be willing to forgive (Matthew 18:21ff—Jesus highlights the permanence of marriage, and calls on His disciples to commit to God's original will and design for it.

The disciples, who have been raised in a context of "easy divorce", recoil at Jesus' words (v. 10). Would it not, they reason, be better not to marry? (v. 10). Jesus concedes that some are called to celibacy, but marriage is still the norm, and therefore faithfulness is still God's will for marriage.

Few things are more important than making every effort to keep our marriages pure and loving. In her book, *How the West Really Lost God*, Mary Eberstadt argues that the decline in the family over the last generation, particularly in the West, has fuelled the decline in religious faith. Numerous surveys have demonstrated that when you weaken marriage and the family, one of the many harmful consequences is weakened faith in God. Furthermore, stable, loving marriages are the healthiest environment for raising children, and they also honour God. As Paul says, a faithful marriage testifies to the greater truth of God's unfailing commitment to His people (Ephesians 5:22–32).

What are the
pressures placed on
marriages today?

What can the
church do to help
strengthen the
marriages of its
members?

Day 44

Read Matthew 19:13–30

Jesus has already given the disciples the example of a small child as a model of those who will enter the kingdom (Matthew 18:1–5). A child's low status reflects the kind of humility that should characterise God's people. The disciples' abrupt rejection of small children who are brought to Jesus shows how little they understand what it means to follow Jesus (vv. 13–15).

In the Sermon on the Mount, Jesus taught the disciples about the character of the righteous: poor, meek, hungry, and mournful (Matthew 5:1–12). In other words, the righteous, like little children, recognise they are essentially needy and dependent. Jesus then taught His followers the path of radical righteousness (Matthew 5:17–48). True righteousness goes beyond outward observance of the law to heartfelt love. Those who practise that righteousness are perfect, or complete (Matthew 5:48).

Now in verses 16 to 22, Matthew gives us a negative example of the kind of childlike faith Jesus has been calling for. Jesus meets a man whose confidence in gaining eternal life rests on a superficial understanding of keeping the commandments. He wonders if there is more he can do (v. 20). Jesus' answer is a challenge to completely reorient one's life by following Him and turning away from reliance on "works" (v. 21). Jesus has already said that we cannot serve both God and money (Matthew 6:24), and so He commands the man to show where his heart truly lies by giving his wealth to the poor and becoming His follower. If he does that, he will demonstrate that he understands the will of God. Then he will be perfect, or complete, making up what he knows is lacking. Sadly, he cannot surrender to this radical call to discipleship, to true righteousness.

As he departs, Jesus says it is impossible for a rich man to be saved. The surprised disciples then ask, "But who can?", because the Jews believe wealth is an indication of God's favour. Jesus replies that while a man cannot save himself, with God "all things are possible" (v. 26). God's way is for us to be the poor and needy who depend on Him. Those who humbly surrender their all to follow Christ will be abundantly rewarded now, and then enter eternal life. Though considered nobodies by worldly standards, they shall be first in His kingdom. Conversely, those who seemed the most "successful", who have relied on themselves, will be the last to find it (v. 30).

The Bible calls on God's people to live righteous lives, but it reminds us that

this is only possible through the power of God. His amazing grace empowers us, first to believe, then to continue willingly and joyfully walking down the costly road of sacrificial love and service.

ThinkThrough

Is Jesus commanding every Christian to "sell your possessions and give to the poor" (v. 21)? If not, how can we faithfully apply what He is calling us to do?

Why is it so hard for a rich person to enter the kingdom of heaven (v. 23)? What does this mean to those of us who live comfortably?

Day 45

Read Matthew 20:1–16

There is a famous story of a British conference on comparative religions, where experts from around the world were discussing whether any one belief was unique to the Christian faith. Some suggested the incarnation, others the resurrection. The debate went on for some time, until C. S. Lewis wandered into the room. He asked, "What's the fuss about?" and on being told, confidently replied, "Oh, that's easy. It's grace."

In chapter 19 we met "the first", a rich, young ruler who was confident of his own righteousness and went away from Jesus sorrowful (vv. 16–22), and then we met "the last", little children of no worldly status who will inherit the kingdom of heaven (vv. 13–15). Bracketed by the saying, "many who are first will be last, and many who are last will be first" (Matthew 19:30; 20:16), Jesus now tells a provocative parable about the grace of God (vv. 1–16).

During those times, many men would be waiting in village squares at dawn in the hope of finding work for the day. This becomes the context for Jesus' parable about a landowner who employs men at different times of the day. What is shocking in the parable is that, irrespective of how many hours the men worked, whether they were employed first or last, all received the same wage (vv. 8–10). Despite the anger of those who worked much longer hours, the master reminds them that nobody has been treated unfairly. His generosity should not be a cause of resentment, but rejoicing (vv. 13–15).

Jesus' simple point is that ultimately, all God's rewards are gifts of grace. **Indeed, it is those who are most aware of their own poverty, and of how little claim they have on God's generosity, who are the most deeply appreciative of the wonder of grace.**

Grace is a concept which is foreign to the human heart. That is why every other world religion has a merit-based view of salvation: do this and you will be saved or reincarnated to a better life. But to a world of sinful men and women, deserving of wrath, only a God of grace brings the hope of eternal salvation.

Do you feel any
sympathy for the
workers who worked
all day? Can you
think of examples
where you might be
tempted to resent
the grace of God?

How would you try
and explain grace
to a non-Christian
friend who thinks
they will go to
heaven because they
have been a good
person?

Day 46

Read Matthew 20:17–34

"Weren't you listening to me?" How many times has a frustrated parent asked this of a child who, when told to do something, immediately went out and did the complete opposite?

It is not surprising that Jesus grew exasperated with the disciples' inability to listen and understand. He has just told a story about grace, demonstrating that the values of the kingdom overturn worldly values (Matthew 20:1–16). Then, in this passage (vv. 17–19), He again reminds them of His imminent humiliating death on a cross. It is incredible, then, that the disciples should turn around and start to argue among themselves about power and greatness (vv. 20–28).

With the support of their mother, James and John ask Jesus to give them the pre-eminent places of authority when He comes into His kingdom (Mark 10:35–37). Of course, they still expected this to be an earthly, political kingdom. Jesus tells them that they have no idea what they are asking for. In particular, they do not understand that in God's kingdom, the path to greatness is through the road of humility and suffering. **There is no crown without a cross.**

The disciples will learn this painful lesson themselves later in their lives:

James will be beheaded (Acts 12:1–2) and John exiled (Revelation 1:9).

The request from the mother of James and John provokes a jealous response from the disciples (v. 24) and so Jesus reminds them that secular models of power simply have no place among God's people (vv. 25–27). His own life modelled this, particularly His self-sacrificial, substitutionary death for them (v. 28). Appropriately, the passage concludes with two beggars crying out for sight (vv. 29–34), and receiving something physically the disciples still lack spiritually.

Much of church history, ancient and contemporary, is a tragic reminder that many Christian leaders have not taken Jesus' words to heart. Too many have clamoured for titles and positions of power for the wrong reasons: there is a persistent temptation to desire the acclaim and benefits that come with such positions. Every minister of the gospel must remain always at the foot of the cross, and be reminded that the cup he or she drinks in Christ's service is the cup of suffering.

Is it wrong to seek positions of power in the church? What makes a Christian understanding of power and leadership radically different from that of the world?

What do you think is the significance of Matthew telling us the story of the two blind beggars (vv. 29–34) immediately after recounting the request by the mother of James and John (vv. 20–28)?

Day 47

Read Matthew 21:1–17

Jesus now completes His climactic journey to Jerusalem and begins His final teaching ministry. Most of it will take place in the temple. He sends two disciples ahead to bring a donkey and her colt to Him. The disciples find things precisely as Jesus had foretold (vv. 2–3). Jesus may be demonstrating His supernatural knowledge of what lies ahead, or He may have made prior agreements.

Jesus rides into Jerusalem on an unbroken animal (the colt, not the mother; see Mark 11:2; Luke 19:30), which placidly obeys its master (vv. 4–7). Everything that Jesus does in these verses demonstrates that He is the Messiah, the true king of Israel. The crowds, part of the large flock of pilgrims who flooded into Jerusalem every year for Passover, greet their King, laying their garments and branches on the road and crying out, "Hosanna", or "save us" (v. 9).

Of course, none of them had any idea of what lay ahead and of how Jesus would be crowned king—not with a sceptre in Jerusalem, but with a crown of thorns on a cross. It is interesting to note that in Hebrew, the word for "temple" is the same as the word for "palace", and so the true king Jesus enters His temple/palace in verse 12.

One section of the temple had become a busy commercial hub, exchanging foreign money for shekels that were acceptable for offerings in the temple and selling thousands of animals for sacrifice, often at extortionate prices (v. 12). The true purpose of the temple as a centre for worship and prayer had been lost (v. 13), and so Jesus dramatically stops this trading. By this act He doesn't just cleanse or reform the temple, but foreshadows its imminent end.

As the centre and focus of worship, the temple had been corrupted. Now, a new centre for life and worship has come: Jesus. **Everything the temple meant for God's people is now fulfilled in Jesus, the true dwelling place of God.** If you wanted to be in God's presence, you went to the temple, but now we come to Jesus. Isaiah envisioned the nations streaming into the temple to come to God (Matthew 2:1–4), but today the nations stream to Jesus. The temple is where the sacrifice to take away sins took place, but Jesus is the sacrifice who took away our sins.

Often people speak of church buildings as being "the house of God". But according to the Bible, what does "the house of God" really mean?

In verse 16, Jesus quotes Psalm 8:2, which speaks of children praising God. By applying this text to himself, what is Jesus telling the Jewish leaders?

Day 48

Read Matthew 21:18–46

We are now in the last week of Jesus' earthly life before He faces the cross, and most of it is spent teaching in the temple. The verbal conflict with the Jewish leaders becomes even more intense. They plague Him with questions designed to trap Him, and as He responds, He exposes the darkness in their hearts and their ultimate spiritual doom.

As Jesus approaches the temple, He sees a fig tree. It bears leaves, which suggests life, but upon closer inspection it is fruitless. Jesus then curses the tree (vv. 18–19). This appears a strange and shocking thing for the Lord to do, until we remember that in the Old Testament, the fig tree was a symbol for Israel (e.g., Jeremiah 24:2–5). This sign prepares us for what will follow in the temple. Like the fig tree, the Jewish nation has proven spiritually barren, and in His debates with the Pharisees, Jesus will similarly pronounce judgment upon them.

In one of the question and answer encounters (vv. 23–27), the chief priests and the elders of the people demonstrate the hardness of their hearts in their refusal to acknowledge that John the Baptist, who proclaimed Jesus as the Messiah, was sent from God, although deep down they knew it to be true. They rejected John, while sinners repented at his preaching.

Jesus then tells two parables exposing the hardness of the Pharisees. The first (vv. 28–32) concerns two sons: one who claims to be obedient but is in fact fruitless (like the fig tree), and another who displays genuine repentance and faith.

The second parable (vv. 33–46) gives a brief review of Jewish history, which was consistently marked by Israel's rejection of God. This rebellion is about to reach its climax in the determination of the Jewish leaders to kill their Messiah, God's Son (vv. 37–39). Again, Jesus alludes to their fruitlessness (v. 43) and pronounces their imminent end (v. 44).

Jesus is foreshadowing the dawn of the new age. The old age was marked by God's dealings with Israel, which failed to be a light to the nations. This age is about to pass away as God's salvation is extended to all people who demonstrate true faith and repentance. **In the end it is not appearances that count, or empty confessions, but the fruit of the Spirit.**

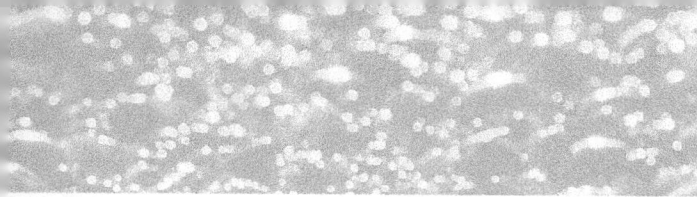

Why do you think Jesus refuses to answer the chief priests and elders' question in verse 27? Is there any lesson here for us in our discussions with people about the gospel?

The appearance of godliness and empty words or confessions is still a danger for today's church. What is the spiritual fruit that God looks for in His people?

Day 49

Read Matthew 22:1–14

We all love weddings. In every culture, they are among the most important and joyful of celebrations. In this passage, God's salvation is portrayed as a wedding banquet. All are invited, but we come on God's terms. There is a dress code for God's banquet.

This is the third of three parables in which Jesus announces a revolution in God's dealings with people. The connections with the previous parables are clear. A vineyard where tenants brutally reject the landowner's servants and kill his son (Matthew 21: 33–45) now gives way to a parable about a wedding feast where the invited guests brutally kill the king's servants. They also reject the king's son by not coming to the feast.

Through the metaphor of a wedding banquet, Jesus again rehearses the history of God's dealings with Israel. The custom in the ancient world was that an invitation was extended to people to attend a wedding. When the food was ready, those who had been invited, and presumably had accepted, were then asked to come.

This banquet is especially important because it is the wedding of the king's son. Despite repeated announcements from the gracious king, his overtures are rejected by those who prefer mammon to God (v. 5) or hate him.

Their violent rejection of the king is again (v. 7; cf. Matthew 21:44) met with judgment, both on them and their city. The invitation is then extended to "the bad as well as the good" (v. 10). Now, anyone who loves and honours the king's son is welcome, even tax collectors and sinners.

The parable ends with a sober warning, as a man is found at the wedding feast dressed inappropriately (v. 11). In other words, while both good and bad are invited to the wedding, once inside the feast you cannot wear the same clothes. John the Baptist told his hearers to bear fruit that expresses true repentance. **We can only attend God's feast on God's terms, which is faith in His Son, expressed in lives of obedience.**

We see here so much of the character of God. We see God's patience in His repeated invitations to come to Him. We see His holiness in His demand for righteousness. We see His wrath on those who repeatedly spurn His love. We see His amazing grace in inviting even the most unworthy into the joy of His salvation.

Think about weddings that you have attended. What makes a wedding banquet such an appropriate metaphor for salvation?

Which part of God's decree for Israel to enter into His salvation also applies to us today?

Day 50

Read Matthew 22:15–46

The verbal battle now resumes. It is striking how traditional enemies—the Pharisees (the more theologically conservative), the Sadducees (the Jewish liberals), and the Herodians (friends of King Herod's family and, therefore, sympathetic to Rome)—now unite to tackle their common enemy, Jesus. Repeatedly, they try to undermine His credibility by asking difficult questions (vv. 15–17).

Most Jews hated the poll tax, which went straight into the Roman coffers (v. 17). It was a daily reminder to them that they were in captivity to a godless foreign power. To condone this tax would be to lose the support of the people. To oppose it was treason. Trapped! Jesus' brilliant answer, "Give back to Caesar what is Caesar's, and to God what is God's" (v. 21), has proven foundational for the church's understanding of its relationship with the secular authorities.

Would Jesus contradict himself? Jesus was probably known to believe in the resurrection of the dead, something that the Sadducees denied. So, in the next question concerning marriage in heaven, they try to use this belief to trap Jesus (vv. 23–28). In His answer, Jesus points out that they are fundamentally mistaken in their understanding of the coming age (vv. 29–32). Using their example of marriage, Jesus says that you can

no more tell what that coming age will be like by looking at this age, than you can predict what a butterfly would become by looking at a caterpillar.

In the final question concerning the greatest commandment (vv. 34–40), Jesus again shows His brilliance by coupling love for God, which is foundational, to love for the neighbour, who is made in God's image, so that from now on, in both Christian thinking and practice the two must remain indivisible.

Jesus asks the last question (vv. 41–46), which forces the Pharisees and the Jews listening in to completely rethink their whole understanding of the most important person in life and history, the Messiah. In authority, power, and glory, He must be greater than any mortal man.

Verbally battered and beaten, the Jewish leaders retreat. In just a few words, Jesus has laid the foundation for a believer's relationship to the government (v. 21), revolutionised our understanding of heaven (vv. 29–32), and taught the essence of our relationship with God and others (vv. 37–40). **No man taught with such wisdom and authority.** Here is a man to listen to, trust, and obey.

What false or foolish notions do people have about heaven? Why do you think the Bible does not tell us everything about what heaven will be like?

Why do you think Jesus insists on making the commands to love God and neighbour indivisible? What might be the repercussions if we tore apart what God has joined together?

Day 51

Read Matthew 23

Matthew 21:18–19 records the cursing of the fig tree. What Jesus announced through a sign, He now makes explicit with His words. "May you never bear fruit again" (Matthew 21:19) finds its solemn echo in Jesus' closing words here: "Look, your house is left to you desolate" (v. 38).

Jesus begins with addressing the crowds and warning them about the Pharisees (vv. 1–12). There are three things to beware of. First, they don't practise what they preach (v. 3). Second, unlike Jesus whose yoke is easy, their many regulations have become an intolerable burden, and all the more so because their teachings lack grace and mercy (v. 4). Finally, they are motivated by pride, seeking to enhance their own status (vv. 5–7). By contrast, the mark of the Christian teacher is humility (vv. 8–12).

Jesus then addresses the religious leaders directly (vv. 13–36), using blunt, accusatory words that pronounce God's judgment upon them ("Woe to you . . ."). These seven words of condemnation (vv. 13, 15, 16, 23, 25, 27, 29) highlight the fact that these men, who were appointed to be teachers of Israel, have actually constructed barriers to salvation by mishandling Scripture, essentially by neglecting what lies at the heart of God's will: justice, mercy, and faithfulness (v. 23).

The climactic seventh woe is the final nail in the Pharisees' coffin (v. 29). For all their pretence at teaching and following God's will, they, like their ancestors, persecute and kill God's messengers. This historical opposition to God will now reach its murderous climax in the Pharisees killing Jesus.

Harsh and uncompromising as these words are, Jesus pronounces them with deep sorrow and regret (v. 37). **The tender image of a hen gathering her chicks is to remind Israel that Jesus came to save, not judge** (Psalm 36:7; 91:4). Tragically, like Israel of old, and like her religious teachers, they have rejected their Messiah. Israel's final desolation is certain, and they will not see their true King again until He comes in His glory (v. 39).

How thankful we should be that we are not under God's condemnation. We have gladly received His salvation. Yet, there is a warning here, too. Never presume upon this salvation. Beware the temptation to hypocrisy and self-seeking. Continue to preach and practise justice, mercy, and righteousness.

What does Jesus mean by His warnings that we not be called Rabbi, Master, Father, or Teacher (vv. 8–10)? Is He prohibiting any titles (e.g., Pastor, Reverend, or Professor)?

Jesus condemns the Pharisees for being religious teachers who neglect justice, mercy, and faithfulness (v. 23). What are some contemporary examples of how we can fall into the same trap?

Day 52

Read Matthew 24:1–44

Jesus' teaching on judgment continues over the next two chapters (Matthew 24–25), although now, He is speaking only to His disciples. All that Jesus says in this section is in answer to two questions His disciples ask Him (v. 3): When will this happen (the temple's destruction)? What will be the sign of your coming?

While some things in this chapter are difficult to understand, Jesus' main points are clear.

First, He warns the disciples not to be deceived by false messiahs or prophets. Then He gives general warnings about this present age. It will be marked by human conflicts, natural disasters, persecution, and the apostasy of many. In the midst of all this, each disciple is called upon to endure faithfully and keep preaching the gospel (vv. 4–14).

Jesus then addresses the issue of the destruction of Jerusalem (vv. 15–28), which occurred in AD 70. It will be an event of great tragedy and suffering, but the disciples must not be deceived into thinking that it heralds the imminent return of Christ to rule (v. 6).

Jesus then answers their question about His coming (vv. 29–31). It will be global, visible, and unmistakable. Importantly, while it will bring judgment for those who reject Jesus, for His followers it is the day of their final salvation, as He gathers them to himself (v. 31).

While the disciples will witness the destruction of Jerusalem (vv. 32–35), no one knows the time of Jesus' coming in glory (v. 36). In the meantime, the disciples are to remain watchful (v. 42).

Tragically, the coming of Jesus will catch most people unawares (vv. 37–41). Just as they are going about their normal, daily routines—having dinner, playing golf, riding the bus—Jesus will return. But it ought not to catch disciples by surprise (vv. 42–51). Only a foolish housekeeper who thinks there is no danger leaves the house unlocked. Similarly, Christians must live each day anticipating Jesus' return and living accordingly.

While there are some disagreements among Bible scholars over the interpretation of particular verses and images, the big message here is: be alert and ready (vv. 42, 44). It is so important that Jesus will repeat it over and over in what follows.

What are some actions that can help us endure to the very end and ensure that our love for God will never grow cold?

Why does Jesus use the example of Noah in His teaching about His Second Coming (vv. 37–39)? What similarities are there between the people of Noah's day and today?

Day 53

Read Matthew 24:45–25:46

Christians know that Jesus will return from heaven to judge the living and the dead. Before that great day, how should we live? Jesus answers this question in four parables, each building on the other.

At the end of the previous section, Jesus told us to be ready because we do not know when He will return (Matthew 24:44). In the first of His four stories, He describes a master who goes away for a while and leaves one of his employees in charge (Matthew 24:45–51). If the employee has performed well, the boss will reward him. If not, he will be thrown out.

The next story describes ten bridesmaids waiting for the groom to arrive at the wedding (Matthew 25:1–13). Like the faithful employee, five know he could be a while and are prepared. Five are not prepared and, upon his arrival, find themselves shut out.

In the third parable, a master entrusts his property to three of his servants (Matthew 25:14–30). Again, the master is away a long time and, as in the earlier parables, we see how the men spend that time. Two use the money the master gives them to make a profit for his kingdom, and are rewarded. Yet, just like there was one faithless employee (Matthew 24:48) and five foolish virgins (Matthew 25:2),

there is an unproductive servant who buries his talent (Matthew 25:24–25). He too is cast out.

We have been told to be ready, and then to be productive in God's service, but what is the profit the master wants from his servants? The final story takes us to judgment day (Matthew 25:31–46). Again, there are two groups of people. What is the difference? It is seen in how they lovingly treat the brothers of Jesus (Matthew 25:40). In Matthew's gospel these "brothers" are Jesus' disciples (cf. Matthew 10:42; 12:48–50; 28:10). **The faithful disciple is the one who uses the resources the Lord has given to him or her to help a brother or sister in need.** Once again, the wicked that do nothing are cast out.

How should we then live? We should use all our resources to bless others, especially God's people, by deeds of love and kindness. This is the profit Jesus wants. These are the ones who are living in the light of Jesus' coming.

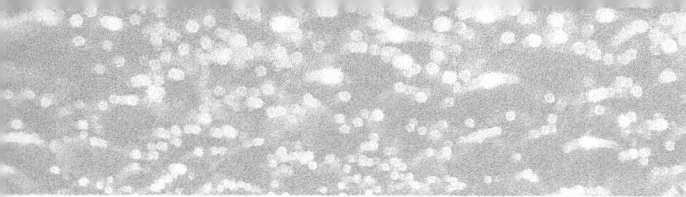

In the light of these parables, what will Jesus look for in the lives of His disciples on judgment day?

Why are the sheep and the goats surprised at the words of the King (Matthew 25:34–45)? What does the parable tell us about Jesus' relationship with His people?

Day 54

Read Matthew 26:1–16

Jesus' death is approaching and we are reminded of that three times in this passage: once by Jesus himself (vv. 1–2), once by the high priest (vv. 3–5), and once by the symbolic act of a woman (vv. 6–13).

Jerusalem was notoriously crowded during Passover. Estimates of 200,000 to several million people have been given by scholars. When visiting Jerusalem, Jesus normally stayed at the home of his close friends, Martha, Mary, and Lazarus, in Bethany, just 3 kilometres away on the south-eastern side of the Mount of Olives.

While there, Jesus attends a dinner hosted by a man called Simon (v. 6). While they are reclining at the table, a woman comes in. Matthew doesn't give us her name, although John tells us that it was Mary, the sister of Martha and Lazarus (John 11:1–3). Although anointing a respected guest is normal, Mary did far more. Matthew emphasises the extravagance of what she did: she used a whole jar of very expensive perfume (v. 7).

The disciples are outraged at the waste (v. 8), claiming the money would have been better spent on the poor. Jesus' reply, "The poor you will always have with you" (v. 11), is not meant to demean care for the poor. His point is that you will be able to tangibly express your love to the poor every day, but you will not be able to physically express your love for Him every day. This woman has grasped something that has continually eluded everyone else: Jesus is going away. **She understands that Jesus has a love for her that will take Him all the way to death and burial** (v. 12).

Indeed, what she has done, Jesus says, will become a model for responding to the gospel (v. 13). Jesus is not telling us that we should always take our most precious item and just give it away; for Abraham it was his only son (Genesis 22), and for a woman of Bethany it was this jar of perfume. Nevertheless, her sacrifice reminds us that when we grasp what Jesus has done for us on the cross, the right response is to love Him in return, lavishly.

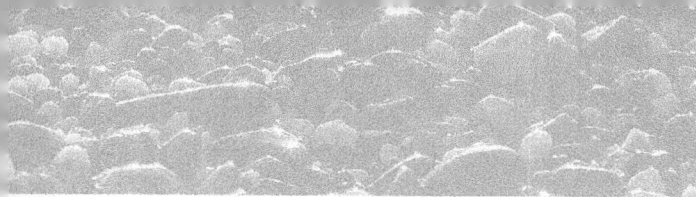

What point do you think Matthew is making by contrasting the woman's anointing of Jesus with Judas' betrayal (vv. 14–16)?

Reflect upon how you have responded to God's love for you displayed in His Son's sacrifice. What has been your "alabaster jar of perfume"?

Day 55

Read Matthew 26:17–35

Jesus has just been anointed with perfume in preparation for His burial (Matthew 26:12). Now He is moving towards His crucifixion. Clearly, He knows precisely what lies ahead of Him, even to the smallest details. Everything in this passage reminds us that ultimately, Jesus died and rose again according to the preordained will and plan of God.

The disciples have asked Jesus where they should make preparations for Him to eat the Passover (v. 17). Of course they will all share in this meal, but unknown to the disciples, this is the last Passover meal Jesus will eat. Jesus then says that His "appointed time is near" (v. 18).

That evening, as they celebrate the Passover, Jesus announces that one of them will betray Him (v. 20). Jesus knows precisely who will betray Him (v.23), for His betrayal and death have been ordained by God (v.24). However, God's ordaining of the betrayal does not lessen the traitor's culpability—"woe to that man who betrays the Son of Man" (v. 24).

The Passover meal included unleavened bread and wine (vv. 26–27). Jesus teaches the disciples the true meaning of the bread and wine. The first Passover in Egypt (Exodus 12) foreshadowed that the Christ would die, His body would be broken, and blood shed, just as one breaks the loaf of bread and pours the wine into the cup.

Finally, Jesus predicts the falling away of the disciples, just as Zechariah 13:7 prophesied (v. 31). Yes, the soldiers and the Jewish priests will hit Jesus, but God will strike the shepherd because this has always been the deliberate plan of God. In particular, Jesus warns Peter of his betrayal and foretells his denial of Jesus, even to the precise moment: "before the cock crows" (v. 34).

Though I can make plans for my future, I can never guarantee their success. But we believe in an almighty God who works all things together for our good, and mysteriously accomplishes this through the wilful, responsible choices and actions of sinful men and women (Genesis 50:20; Romans 8:28). Only this sovereign God is worth entrusting your future to. **He knew you before you knew Him. He has ordained good for you, namely your sanctification and glorification.** What God wills, He accomplishes (Isaiah 14:27; 46:11).

Read this passage again. What other examples can you find that demonstrate that Jesus knew exactly what the future held for Him?

Reflect upon Matthew's description of the Passover meal (vv. 26–29). How does it help us to understand our observance of the Lord's Supper?

Day 56

Read Matthew 26:36–56

Having eaten the Passover meal, Jesus and the disciples go up the Mount of Olives into the garden called Gethsemane, which means "oil press" (v. 36). It is very late, so the garden would be quiet and deserted, which is why Jesus liked it so much.

Jesus prays and Matthew describes the depth of Jesus' grief: "My soul is overwhelmed with sorrow to the point of death" (v. 38). This is not figurative language. His anguish was so deep it would have killed Him (cf. Hebrews 5:7). Why? Because He knew He was about to drink the cup of God's wrath for the sins of the world (cf. Jeremiah 25:15). Despite His heartbreak, Jesus knew there could be no other way, and prays, "Yet not as I will, but as you will" (v. 39).

His determination to do God's will thus strengthened, Jesus meets the soldiers. At the head of the crowd is Judas, "one of the Twelve" (v. 47), says Matthew, just to emphasise the depth of his betrayal. Judas had seen Jesus calm a storm, raise the dead, feed 5,000 men, walk on water, and countless other signs and wonders. It beggars belief that he would do such a thing to a loving friend and master. But it gets worse.

"Now the betrayer had arranged a signal with them" (v. 48). It might have been dark in Gethsemane, which probably explains why Judas felt it necessary to identify Jesus. But the signal he gives is the most intimate and affectionate expression of love and friendship between human beings: the kiss (vv. 48–49).

Finally, Jesus points out the cowardice of this crowd who had ample opportunity to arrest Him publicly, but now come to Him like He was a common rebel. Yet, as we have seen, all this is done exactly as stated in the Old Testament, so that "the Scriptures be fulfilled that say it must happen in this way" (vv. 54, 56).

"Am I leading a rebellion?" (v. 55). Do you see the great irony here? In a sense, the answer is "yes". **There is something deeply subversive about a kingdom which calls for repentance and radical purity, and whose weapons are deeds and words of love.** Jesus was a rebel, who by drinking that cup made possible the greatest rebellion of all: the revolution of the human heart.

Since Jesus knew that He was going to the cross, how can we explain His prayer for the cup to be taken from Him (v. 39)? What does this tell us about Jesus? What does Jesus' petition in the garden teach us about prayer?

How can you explain the betrayal of Judas? What does it tell us about human sin?

Day 57

Read Matthew 26:57–75

Courtroom dramas continue to captivate people, whether real-life or in the movies. It is the battle for justice, the tussle between prosecution and defence, and the uncertainty of the jury's verdict. Now, as Jesus is brought before the Sanhedrin, Matthew places two trials side-by-side. Two men who are best friends stand before hostile audiences and are called upon to stand firm and make a true confession. For both, it is a life-and-death decision. The men are Jesus and Peter.

In between the trials of Jesus, Matthew mentions how Peter warmed himself by a fire (see Luke 22:55; John 18:18). He wants us to contrast the trials these two men will face.

Normally, in a trial, evidence is presented, then an impartial judge assesses it and pronounces a verdict and sentence. However, in Jesus' trial, the verdict and sentence has already been decided (vv. 59–60). The only accusation is that Jesus threatened to destroy the temple (v. 61), a blatant distortion of His prophecy in chapter 24 (see also John 2:19; Mark 14:58). Then, when asked if He is the Christ, Jesus calmly refuses to deny it (vv. 63–64).

Peter's trial takes place in the courtyard outside (v. 58). In Jesus' trial, all the witnesses were false (v. 60), but here, there are numerous eyewitnesses who all speak with one voice: this man was with Jesus (vv. 69, 71, 73). Jesus openly admits He is God's Son (v. 64), while Peter denies emphatically that he is a disciple (vv. 70, 72, 74). In the end, Jesus is accused of blasphemy because He claimed to be God (vv. 64–65), while Peter himself blasphemes, calling down curses on his own head (v. 74).

"Immediately a cock crowed" (v. 74) after Peter's third denial, and Jesus' prophecy was fulfilled. In that awful moment, Peter saw what a boastful, cowardly, faithless man he was, and wept bitterly (v. 75).

We may never stand trial like Peter did, but we are regularly called upon to confess that we belong to Jesus. Although this is the last mention of Peter in this gospel, it is not the end of his story. For Peter, and for us, there may be failure and bitter tears, but with Jesus there is also forgiveness and restoration.

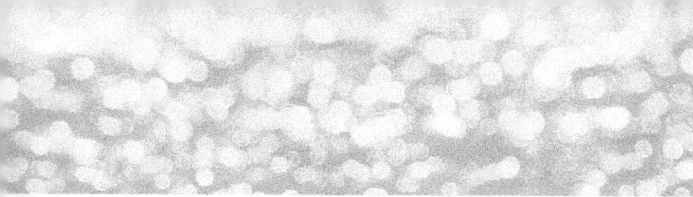

ThinkThrough

When facing His accusers, why does Jesus sometimes answer and sometimes remain silent?

Can you think of times when we are called upon to confess that we are disciples of Jesus? On such occasions, what causes us to fear?

Day 58

Read Matthew 27:1–26

F ew things anger us more than the miscarriage of justice—when the guilty escape punishment, or the innocent are condemned. The innocence of Jesus is an important theme in these final chapters of Matthew's gospel.

First, Judas, His betrayer, affirms Jesus' innocence (vv. 1–4). Overcome with remorse, he returns the money of his betrayal to the religious leaders. Judas confesses his guilt in betraying an innocent man, but the leaders' response is callous: "What is that to us?" Jesus' legal innocence or guilt is irrelevant to them; they want Him dead. As Jesus said about these men: "Woe to you . . . you have neglected the more important matters of the law—justice, mercy and faithfulness" (Matthew 23:23).

Matthew now completes the story of Judas. Matthew has presented us with two men who betrayed Jesus: Judas, who handed Jesus over (26:47–50); and Peter, who denied Him (26:69–75). Both are deeply sorrowful (26:75; 27:3). One commits suicide (v. 5), while the other is restored (John 21:15–17). What is the difference?

In 2 Corinthians 7:10, Paul writes, "Godly sorrow brings repentance that leads to salvation and leaves no regret, but worldly sorrow brings death". Godly sorrow does not drive you to the hangman's noose but to the Saviour and the cross, the place of repentance and forgiveness.

Matthew then briefly describes Jesus' formal trial before the Gentile governor, Pontius Pilate (vv. 11–26). Again we see the determination of the chief priests and elders to have Jesus killed. Pilate offers the Jews a choice: the blatantly guilty Jesus Barabbas (Barabbas literally means "son of the father"), or the innocent Jesus Christ, the Son of the Father. They cry for the guilty to be released and the innocent to be executed. Pilate's wife affirms Jesus' righteousness (v. 19). Then Pilate himself affirms that Jesus has done nothing wrong (v. 23–24).

The innocent is punished while the guilty goes free. However, the good news is that through this terrible miscarriage of justice, God has worked to set us all free. It has been suggested that the cross Jesus died on was intended for Barabbas, but he was released. **In a sense, the cross was intended for us. We deserved to die there, but in His love for us Jesus died in our place.** We have walked free because Jesus drank the cup of God's wrath for us (Matthew 26:42; Job 21:20; Isaiah 51:17).

What can we learn about sorrow and repentance from the stories of Peter and Judas?

"Jesus died for me". When did this great truth first become real to you? How does it affect the way you live today?

Day 59

Read Matthew 27:27–50

"For the joy that was set before him he endured the cross, scorning its shame" (Hebrews 12:2). While a terribly painful form of execution, crucifixion was designed to maximise shame. Crucified in public places (like the top of a hill), the dying criminal was the object of ridicule. Yet, through their taunts, Jesus' enemies ironically proclaim the truth.

First, the soldiers mock Jesus. They dress Him in make-believe royal robes, place a crown of thorns on His head, and thrust a pretend-sceptre into His hand. In cruel mockery they hail Him as king. The great irony is that they are speaking more truly than they could have imagined. He is a king—the King—and He is going to receive His kingdom (vv. 27–31).

As Matthew describes the events of Jesus' crucifixion, so much of what happens fulfils Psalms 22 and 69: the dividing of His clothes (v. 35; Psalm 22:18), the insults hurled at Him (vv. 37–44; Psalms 22:7, 69:9–12), the cry of desolation (v. 46; Psalm 22:1), and giving Him vinegar to drink (v. 48; Psalm 69:21). The Jewish leaders taunt Jesus, saying, "He saved others . . . but he can't save himself!" (v. 42), however the irony is that in choosing not to save himself, He is saving all of mankind.

Throughout this entire ordeal, Jesus has remained silent to the taunting. Now He speaks, and in Matthew's gospel, the crucified Jesus speaks just one time. Quoting Psalm 22:1, He expresses, in a voice of deep emotion, His sense of divine abandonment. Of course, the God Jesus called out to was "My God", but as He bore God's wrath, the agony of separation from the Father was indescribable.

As if to reflect this, God sends a veil of darkness over all the land. In the words of Frederick Bruner, "In the darkness the natural world puts on, as it were, widow's weeds, dresses in dark clothing, and goes into mourning, for here the human world has committed its most heinous crime."

Jesus bore the shame of sin, judgment, and punishment so we could receive glory.

He suffered thirst so we could drink from the well of salvation. He died in darkness so we could live in the light. He was abandoned by God so we could be reconciled to Him.

God forsaking God. No man can understand that!" (Martin Luther). What can we understand about our salvation from the cry of the Lord Jesus (v. 46), and what remains unfathomable?

Make a list of all that has been achieved for us by Jesus' atoning death on the cross. Then spend a few moments praising and thanking Him.

Day 60

Read Matthew 27:51–66

The Jewish leaders have spoken about Jesus: He is a blasphemer (Matthew 26:65). Pilate has spoken: He is innocent (Matthew 27:24). In mockery, the crowds have spoken (Matthew 27:20, 27–31, 41–44). Yet, up to this point, apart from the darkness (Matthew 27:45) the response from God seems muted. But now, Matthew concludes his account of the death of Jesus with the powerful voice of God.

We say that actions speak louder than words, and in this passage God speaks powerful action words. One feature of the language of the Greek New Testament is what is called the "divine passive". The passive voice is used to express God's action. Here we read that the curtain of the temple was torn in two. Who tore it? God. The earth was shaken (v. 51). By whom? God. The rocks were split open. Who smashed them? God. The tombs were opened and many holy people who had died were raised (v. 52). Again, this is God's doing.

God tore the curtain in the temple to announce that we now have full access to His presence. There is no longer a forbidden "Most Holy Place" (Hebrews 10:19–22). This occurred the moment Jesus breathed His last. Then God raised some of the dead to announce that death had been defeated and we will all rise from the dead one day. While the graves were split open, the raising of the dead actually took place "after Jesus' resurrection" (v. 53), because Christ must rise first (see 1 Corinthians 15:20).

By these two events God is showing us the real significance of the death of Jesus. It means the way is now open for us all to come to God (Hebrews 10:19–20), and it means the promise of our bodily resurrection (1 Corinthians 15:20, 23). Of course, our rising from the dead will happen at the end of time, but like the preview of a coming attraction, God raises some of the dead right away.

How should we respond to God speaking? Matthew tells us through the words of a Gentile soldier who, while being part of the execution squad, witnessed all these events. He confesses, "Surely he was the Son of God!" (v. 54).

Whose voice are you listening to? Is it the taunts of the Jewish leaders and others like them today? Is it the lies and fabrications of the Pharisees (vv. 62–66) and of modern sceptics? Or is it the voice of the living God, who speaks words of truth, life, and hope?

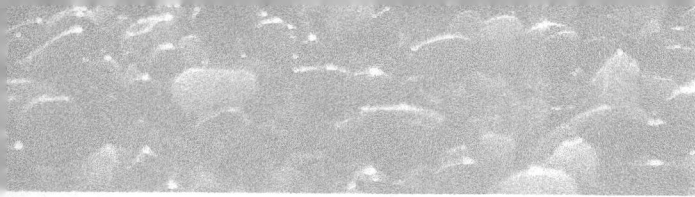

"The curtain of
the temple was
torn in two from
top to bottom"
(v. 51). What are
the implications of
this event for how
men and women
approach God?

What do you
think caused the
centurion to reach
the conclusion that
Jesus was God's son
(v. 54)?

Day 61

Read Matthew 28:1–15

How can we be sure that the foundation of the Christian faith is a solid one? How can we be sure that Jesus is God's Son and the world's Saviour? How can we be confident of our eternal destiny? The answer is the resurrection.

On the Sunday morning after Jesus' death, two women, both named Mary, go to the tomb (v. 1). Nobody expected Jesus to rise from the dead. The last we heard of the disciples was in Matthew 26:56, when "all the disciples deserted him and fled".

"Suddenly" (v. 2 NLT) everything changes, forever. After an earthquake, an angel appears with the momentous news, "He is not here . . ." (v. 6). Matthew then gives us three reasons why we can believe in the truth of the resurrection.

First, "He has risen, just as he said" (v. 6). Jesus told His followers repeatedly that He would rise from the dead (Matthew 16:21; 17:9, 23; 20:19; 26:32; 27:63). Jesus never lies and He has the power to accomplish whatever He promises. We have seen these truths demonstrated repeatedly throughout the gospel.

Second, Jesus met them (v. 9). Jesus knew we would not believe the women's testimony alone. Thus He appeared, not just to the women, but also to the disciples and many others, again and again. They physically touched Him and spoke with Him (Mark 16:14; Luke 24:13–43; John 20:19–29; Acts 1:3–11; 10:40; 1 Corinthians 15:3–7).

Thirdly, Matthew describes the lie the Jewish leaders were spreading, that Jesus' body had been stolen (v. 13). It should have been the easiest thing in the world for them to disprove the resurrection: just produce His corpse. But they couldn't, because the tomb was empty.

There was no way that, following torture and execution, Jesus could have just revived in the tomb and then appeared in perfect health before others. Nor was it possible that the disciples had simply stolen the body. Nor could it be that they merely believed He had risen metaphorically. No, Jesus said He would rise from the dead. He appeared before many people. He conquered death and rose bodily from the tomb.

By raising Jesus from the dead, God has spoken. Jesus said He was the Son of God. Now, God says, "Yes! He's my Son." Jesus had said that He was the Saviour of the world. Now God says, "Yes, I forgive your sins because my Son died for you."

Since this is true, there is nothing more important than for every single person to follow the risen Lord Jesus.

_____

_____

_____

_____

_____

Do you think it would have made a difference to our faith if Jesus had not risen from the dead?

What excuses have you heard people give for not believing in the resurrection of Jesus?

Day 62

Read Matthew 28:16–20

This is the dramatic conclusion of Matthew's gospel, and the final words of the risen Christ. I love to read missionary biographies, the encouraging and challenging stories of men and women who have obediently gone out to make disciples of all nations. In missionary writings over the past 200 years, no Scripture is quoted more often, or has been more influential, than Matthew 28:18–20.

The Extreme Claim: All Authority (v. 18). Many people object to evangelising, saying that we have no right to invite others to change their religion. Jesus, however, has the right, because He has all authority. He has authority over every moment of every day, and over every creature in heaven and on earth, and over every single man, woman, and child. Since He exercises all authority, He has the right to be worshipped and obeyed by every single person.

The Extreme Command: All Nations (v. 19). Jesus' great command highlights four activities we should be involved in: going, making, baptising, and teaching. There is just one command: "make disciples". The rest of the verse explains the where and the how of disciple-making. As we go out into the world, whether near or far, we are to evangelise to people and teach them to become mature disciples.

The Extreme Comfort: Always (v. 20). Matthew's gospel closes with words similar to those with which it opened: "'and they will call him Immanuel' (which means 'God with us')" (Matthew 1:23). Here, this Immanuel promises to be true to His name and be with us until the end of the age. The underlying assumption behind His word of comfort is that it will be impossible to fulfil this command without Him. As the Lord was with Peter, James and John, Paul and Barnabas, William Carey, Hudson Taylor, and many others, so He will be with us as we continue to make disciples, until the end of the age.

No one can say, "The Lord hasn't called me". Today we have heard the Lord's command. Some will leave the comforts of home and go where Christ is not known. Most of us will make disciples where we live. But having heard the good news of Jesus, we must now make Him known to the world.

How would you define "disciple-making"?

What is your church doing right now to obey Jesus' command? Is there room for improvement?

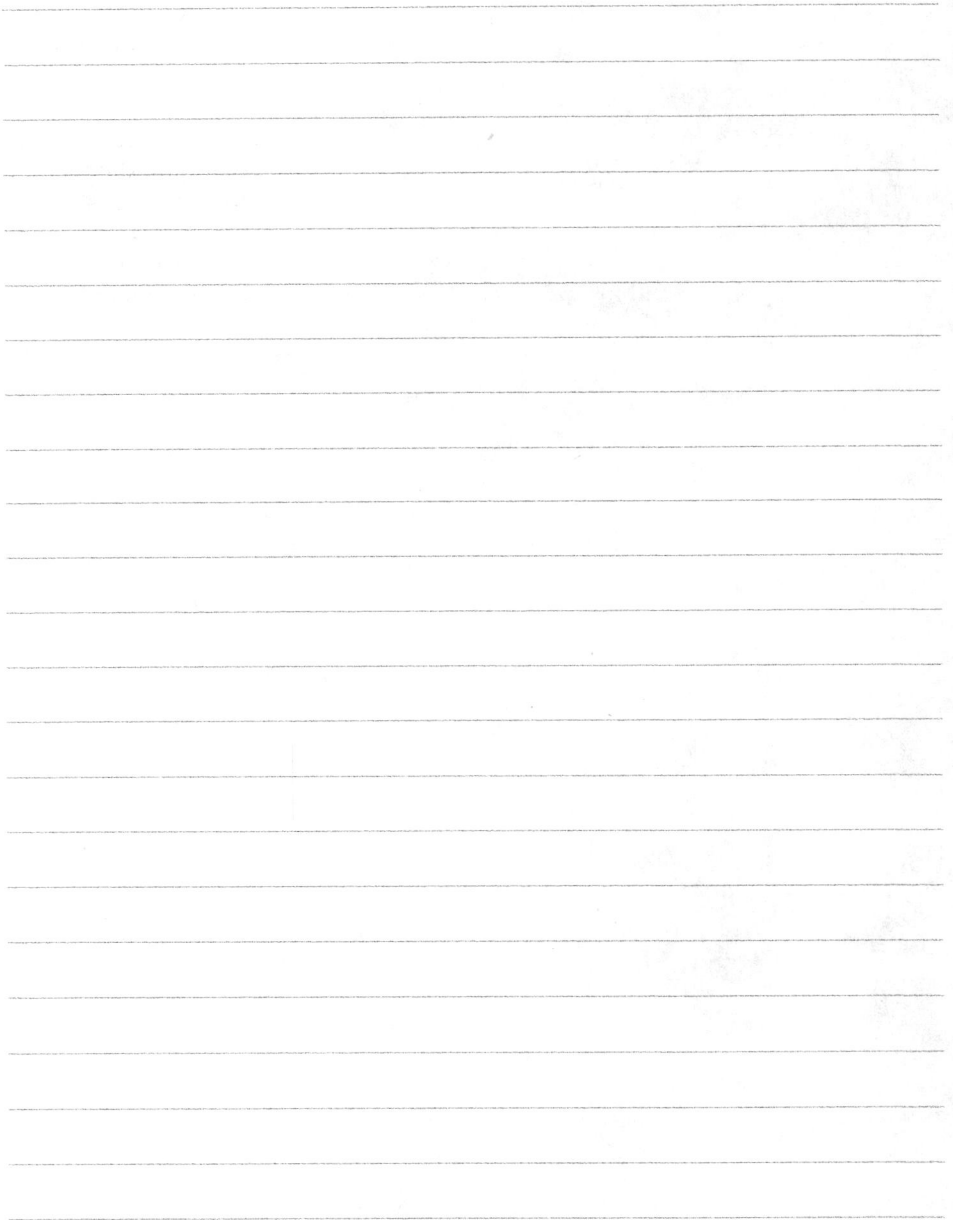

ABOUT THE PUBLISHER

Discovery House Publishing™
produces a wide array of premium
and quality resources that focus on Scripture,
show reverence for God and His Word,
demonstrate the relevance of vibrant faith,
and equip and encourage you to draw closer
to God in all seasons of your life.

Discovery House
Publishing™

NOTE TO THE READER

We invite you to share your response to the message
of this book by writing to us at:

**5 Pereira Road #07-01
Asiawide Industrial Building
Singapore 368025**

or sending an email to:

dhpsingapore@dhp.org

For more information about the *Journey Through* series,
please visit us online at:

journeythrough.org